"Surrounded by complex issues ('human rights,' 'science and religion,' 'secularism,' 'New Atheism,' and many more), it is hard to understand what's going on, what the important thinkers are saying and what a thinking Christian might make of it all. Nick Spencer carves out a clear path through the jungle, helping us to see how we got here in the first place and how we might move forward in faith and wisdom."

N. T. Wright, Research Professor of New Testament and Early Christianity, University of St Andrews

"This book weaves together two topics that are rarely without controversy: Christianity and its critical role in the evolution of democratic states in Europe and beyond. Spencer details an honest critique and well-articulated trajectory of Christianity and its place in our modern-day understanding of values, identity and citizenship. His deep understanding is unparalleled, as it's been throughout the last decade at Theos. Spencer helps us to think clearly about issues that remain critical in our appreciation of modern-day debates around who we are and how this is deeply intertwined with a strong, robust and vital Christian history. All readers, whatever their religious, non-religious or political persuasions, will discover a stimulating book in both its scholarly credentials and scope."

Sughra Ahmed, Chair, Islamic Society of Britain

THE EVOLUTION
OF THE WEST

Expanded Edition

THE EVOLUTION
OF THE WEST

Expanded Edition

How Christianity Has Shaped Our Values

Nick Spencer

WJK WESTMINSTER
JOHN KNOX PRESS
LOUISVILLE • KENTUCKY

© 2016, 2018 Nick Spencer

First published in Great Britain in 2016
by the Society for Promoting Christian Knowledge

Expanded edition

Louisville, Kentucky

18 19 20 21 22 23 24 25 26 27—10 9 8 7 6 5 4 3 2 1

Scripture quotations marked NIV are from The Holy Bible, New International Version
(Anglicized edition). Copyright © 1979, 1984, 2011 by Biblica (formerly International
Bible Society). Used by permission of Hodder & Stoughton Publishers, an Hachette
UK company. All rights reserved. "NIV" is a registered trademark of Biblica (formerly
International Bible Society).

Book design by Sharon Adams
Cover design by Mark Abrams

Library of Congress Cataloging-in-Publication Data

Names: Spencer, Nick, 1973- author.
Title: Evolution of the West / Nick Spencer.
Description: Expanded edition. I Louisville, KY : Westminster John Knox Press, 2018.
  I Includes bibliographical references and index. I
  Identifiers: LCCN 2017049190 (print) I LCCN 2017051149 (ebook) I ISBN
  9781611648560 (ebk.) I ISBN 9780664263836 (pbk. : alk. paper)
Subjects: LCSH: Values--Religious aspects. I Church and the world. I
  Christian ethics. I Christianity.
Classification: LCC BR115.W6 (ebook) I LCC BR115.W6 S58 2018 (print) I DDC 270--dc23
LC record available at https://lccn.loc.gov/2017049190

Our past is sedimented in our present.

–Charles Taylor, *A Secular Age*

Contents

Acknowledgments

———◆•◆•◆———

I have learned more than I can chart from more people than I can remember over the last ten years at Theos. To single people out would be invidious and risky, as I would almost certainly forget and offend some. I would, however, like to pay particular thanks to all my colleagues at Theos, but most especially Paul W., Paul B., Elizabeth, Ben, and Jennie, who have been an inspiration, as well as a good laugh. I would also like to thank John Langlois and Bill Latimer for their generous support and encouragement, and Henry van Oosterom for his excellent work in compiling the index.

This book is dedicated to another Paul—Paul Oliver—without whom I doubt whether I would ever have written a word.

Nick Spencer

Introduction

1

For the last ten years I have worked for Theos, a Christian think tank based in Westminster. Theos was launched in November 2006, which, by some quirk of divine humor, was a month after Richard Dawkins's *The God Delusion* was published. The so-called New Atheists were sweeping all before them, as the world reeled from the sometimes impertinent, sometimes horrific intrusion of religious commitment into public life, and in consequence temperatures rose and for a time the ordinary habits of civility stood aside and sinister metaphors and cardboard caricatures spread through discourse like a virus, or maybe a meme.

> We understand that the faithful live in an inspissated [it means "thickened" or "congealed," apparently] gloaming of incense and obfuscation, through the swirls of which it is hard to see anything clearly, so a simple lesson in semantics might help to clear the air for them on the meanings of "secular," "humanist" and "atheist."

So wrote A. C. Grayling, a New Atheist understudy, in an essay that greeted the launch of Theos with less than complete joy.

The general foot-stamping continued for a while, reaching a high or perhaps low point with a notorious atheist bus campaign that inspiringly entreated people to "stop worrying and start enjoying your life," to which Theos made a small contribution in the naïve hope that it would at least encourage people to think about the meaning of life. Even at that time, however, in the early days of this new movement, we heard from atheists who were disquieted by the noisiness of their compatriots and who, while agreeing wholeheartedly with their rejection of all things divine, quietly wished they would avoid sounding quite so sophomoric and self-righteous when doing so.

Silent disquiet rumbled on but eventually more and more atheists were prepared to say "Not in my name." The editor of *New Humanist*, the magazine of the Rationalist Association in Britain, wrote an editorial observing that Dawkins provided "a case study in how not to do it," pointing out that blanket condemnations of religious groups were morally dubious (as well as counterproductive); that religious believers were in fact no less intelligent than non-believers; and that secularism did not mean excluding religious believers from public life. The writer Alain de Botton published a book titled *Religion for Atheists*, which suggested atheists were better stealing from religion than mocking it. Atheist churches opened up in North London, complete with sermons and singing. The atheist analytic philosopher, Thomas Nagel, ventured to suggest that the "materialist neo-Darwinian conception of nature" failed to explain the origins of life, human consciousness, intentionality, meaning and value, and was "almost certainly false." John Gray, a disarmingly honest British atheist philosopher, repeatedly demolished self-satisfied humanistic atheism with aplomb, attacking it with precisely the same Darwinian weapons that it had used on God: "Atheism and humanism . . . seem to be conjoined when in fact they are at odds . . . a type of atheism that refused to revere humanity would be a genuine advance."

At some point, the New Atheism storm finally seemed to pass over the horizon, and the more reflective, self-critical, and realistic voices were again heard in atheist thought. Writing ten years after Theos's launch, it feels a little easier to say you are a Christian in public without others instantly claiming that that clearly means you are the unwitting host for virus more dangerous than smallpox.

Storms often leave a trail of destruction, scattering debris in their wake, and although this one may have passed, or at least have lessened in intensity and extent, it has left a lingering sense that Christianity was more or less tolerable. At a personal level, it advocated certain practices that appeared to help foster psychological well-being. Communally, it helped feed, clothe, and support many people in need, as well as providing a focus point for much community activity. Creatively, it clearly lay somewhere behind many of the greatest artistic achievements of European civilization. In as far as its allegedly innately violent tendencies could be defused, and providing it was kept in the leisure category of our lives and prevented from bothering the adults as they got on with the business of running the world, Christianity was sufferable.

Such an approach necessitated a certain historic logic that could sometimes border on outright amnesia. According to this narrative, modern people lived by Enlightenment values that were developed in the Enlightenment period by Enlightenment philosophers who not only had no discernible intellectual connection with those who went before them, but who worked in the teeth of opposition from obscurantist and often violent churchmen. The more generous treatments of the same theme extended the historic borders, back to the Renaissance when human dignity and nobility were first discovered, and forward to the post-war period when human rights were established and welfare states set up. And the most generous treatments would acknowledge the presence of the odd, usually dissenting, Christian thinker or activist in this mix. Nonetheless, the central narrative was the same: that of slow but steady secular emancipation.

One doesn't need to go quite as far as Christopher Hitchens's claim that religion poisons everything to witness such amnesia. Jonathan Israel, a supremely erudite historian of the Enlightenment, is quoted making a comparably sweeping and dismissive statement in chapter 1 below. "What has 'theology' ever said that is of the smallest use to anybody?" asked Richard Dawkins rhetorically, seemingly unaware of the early Church's debates about personhood and what it meant for human nature and dignity, a quality that underlies almost everything else. "The Church of England switched only recently from being the Tory party at prayer to being stoutly leftwing," according to newspaper columnist Simon Jenkins, a statement that is both wrong (Church of England congregations are disproportionately right-of-center) and wrong again (the Church of England hierarchy made an oddly unified move to the left around the turn of the nineteenth century). The list could go on but the point should be clear: sometimes subtly, sometimes accidentally, sometimes egregiously the role of Christianity in forming Western values that we hold dear is rewritten or forgotten.

Amnesia of this nature is not simply a cause of concern to Christians. Indeed, if anything it is a bigger issue for historians as it illustrates how we can lose the ability of hearing the music of the past in its own key.

The past, at least in Europe, was Christian—a statement that has no hidden implications as to whether the present is or the future will be. People thought in Christian and spoke in Christian and reasoned in Christian, even as the public square became ever more plural. Belief was ubiquitous, shaping even the minority who did not believe. In the words of the historian turned Conservative politician, John Redwood:

> Whenever a man took up his pen and attempted to write about the weather, the seasons, the structure of the earth, the constitution of the heavens, the nature of political society, the organization of the Church, social morality or ethics he was by definition taking up his pen to write about God.

Redwood is here writing of early modern Europe but the sentiments, albeit increasingly diluted, apply well into the nineteenth century and even into the twentieth. In the words of Samuel Moyn, whose book on human rights is explored in chapter 9, "the trouble . . . is not so much that Christianity accounts for nothing, as that it accounts for everything." Secular moderns often have a tin ear when it comes to the religiosity of history, and it matters.

2

This book comprises a collection of essays, reviews, and lectures written and/or delivered in ten years at Theos, although subsequently revisited and revised substantially, alongside a number of essays that appear here for the first time. I have decided to dispense with foot/endnotes for the most part as the essays are not intended to be scholarly pieces. Together, they are an attempt to hear the past in its own key, rather than instinctively transposing it into one with which we are familiar, and comfortable, today. However, the book is more than simply a collection that shows how Christian Europe's past was, a fact that may be discerned from the list of topics covered—dignity, nationhood, law, democracy, humanism, atheism, science, secularism, ethics, rights, welfare, capitalism—none of which is exactly irrelevant to where we are today. *The Evolution of the West* hopes to speak as much to present concerns as to past ones.

There is a significant danger in doing this, which may be illustrated with reference to the BBC comedy show *Goodness Gracious Me.* A recurring sketch in this sees a young British Indian in vexed conversation with his bombastic father. In one scene the young man sits on the sofa in the front room watching Trooping the Colour on TV. His father sits behind a magazine paying no attention to the program. The young man sighs admiringly. "The Queen looks nice doesn't she?"

"Nice? Of course nice," his father puts down the magazine. "Because she's Indian."

"What? The Queen?" the son asks, incredulous. It's too late to stop the father, however. He's off.

"All of them. The whole Royal Family—INDIAN! Think about it," he tries to persuade his skeptical son.

> Descended from Queen Victoria, Empress of India, so Indian. Look at them. They all live in the same family house together—INDIAN! All work in the family business—INDIAN! All have arranged marriages—INDIAN! They all have sons, daughters no good—INDIAN! Children live with their parents until they are married—INDIAN! What more do you want? You want them to put on turban and charm snakes out of baskets?

This is a temptation for those Christians writing about what the modern world owes to Christianity. "Rights—CHRISTIAN! Read 1 Corinthians 9:4. Science—CHRISTIAN! Read 1 Kings 4:33. Ethics—CHRISTIAN! Read Psalm 14:1. Law—CHRISTIAN! Read Deuteronomy 4:1." There is no end of cheap proof-texting that can show how the West owes everything to Christianity—or rather everything it currently holds dear. It's an exercise not only scripturally and theologically shallow but every bit as historically tone deaf as any New Atheist polemic. If Christians of the present think Christians of the past unanimously spent their time campaigning volubly for democracy, welfare, rights, and the Scientific Revolution, they should spend some time reading the Christians of the past.

Samuel Moyn makes this point well when writing of the origins of human rights. "The truth is," he observes, "that Europe and therefore the modern world drew nearly everything from Christianity in the long term." "Without Christianity, our commitment to the moral equality of human beings is unlikely to have come about." But this by itself, he goes on to remark, "had no bearing on most forms of political equality—whether between Christians and Jews, whites and blacks, civilized or savage, or men and women." Moreover, "it would be fictitious retrospectively to edit the long and tumultuous history of Europe, as if everything we liked about the outcomes were due to its hegemonic religion, while the rest was an unfortunate accident or someone else's fault." In other words, Christianity has played a big role in this show—indeed it has played the lead for much of the last 1,500 years—but the play has been no mere soliloquy, and the lead has had a somewhat ambiguous relationship with the overall plotline.

That this is the argument of this collection should be signalled both by some of its contents—rarely, for example, are "atheism" or the "secular self" counted among Christianity's great, intended gifts to the West—and by its title. "Evolution" is popularly understood as a smooth, linear, even intentional progress line from the simple to the complex, from *Homo habilis* on the left to *Homo sapiens*, dignified and usually carrying a spear, on the right. In reality, it is nothing of the kind, being more akin to a circuitous path marked by circumstance and accident rather than a smooth, gradual parabola; a tree whose branches reach out in many different directions rather than a flagpole whose only way is up.

Although one should always be careful about pushing metaphors—not least evolutionary ones—too far, or on to schemes where they have limited place, it is not stretching evidence or credibility to breaking point to see the intellectual development of the European mind and values, and the Christian influence thereon, in this way. There has been continuity and progress. Yesterday did turn into today, and today is clearly different from yesterday. But the transition from one to the other is complex, convoluted, and full of dead ends, accidents, coincidences, and unintended consequences. The tree of Western values did grow in Christian soil but it would be a mistake to imagine that soil had some precise blueprint for what the tree would eventually look like.

3

This invites one further but important question. The debate over how random evolution is has been a long-standing and intemperate one. Accordingly, using the metaphor of evolution to describe the development of European values, and Christianity's role in that, might be taken to imply that the process under discussion has been entirely arbitrary. Were we to rewind the clock 2,000 or so years and run history again, we would find that, even were Christianity to have established itself as the dominant intellectual and cultural "imaginary" of the continent, everything would have "evolved" differently: no human dignity, no humanism, no rule of law, no concept of rights, no scientific revolution—a wholly different ethical, social, and political world.

Such might be the conclusion were the idea of unrepeatable randomness well established in evolutionary circles. That is certainly how some, such as the late Stephen Jay Gould, thought of it. "If you could rewind the tape of life," he once remarked, in a more analog age, "erasing what actually happened and let it run again, you'd get a different [result] each time."

And yet there is another way of looking at the process, which shows it to be rather less haphazard and perhaps even opens up a strangely apt theological angle on the subject. This way lies in the seeming ubiquity of convergence—"the recurrent tendency of biological organization to arrive at the same 'solution' to a particular need." Biologically, this is now widely recognized: eyes (both camera and compound), wings, legs, claws, teeth, brains, tool-use, agriculture, and much else besides have evolved time and time and time again. Given the initial conditions in which life on earth evolves, there are, it seems, only so many ways of feeding, fighting, fleeing, and reproducing. For all the randomness involved in the process, there are certain inherent invisible conditions and constraints and contours that shape it toward ends that, if not predictable, are certainly probable. In the words of evolutionary paleobiologist Simon Conway Morris, whose book *Life's Solution* illustrates this principle with admirable force and clarity, "the evolutionary routes are many, but the destinations are limited."

Perhaps that is a fruitful way of looking at the evolution of Western values. Given the Christian "constraints"—the ideas, convictions, commitments, "imaginaries" (a term we shall return to when discussing Charles Taylor's *A Secular Age* in chapter 10)—within which Western culture developed, certain paths, directions, and even possibly destinations became if not predictable, certainly possible, and maybe probable. From the understanding of human nature, identity, community, and destiny inspired by the life and teaching of Jesus Christ, and by the reflections and practices of his early followers, certain further commitments to human dignity, "humanism," the rule and significance of law, nationhood, and "political" authority were generated. The innumerable political vicissitudes in the afterlife of the Western Roman empire took these commitments in different directions, as did the various Renaissances—Carolingian, Aristotelian, Italian—that followed them, and these various combinations of Christian commitments and historical circumstances in their turn generated still further ideas that, in time, germinated political and religious actions and reactions—such as atheism and secularism—that came to reshape early modern Europe. From one perspective it all looks rather a bit like Joseph Heller's rubbish-bag of random coincidences blown open by the wind, but on closer inspection the bag had certain specific contents and the wind was blowing in a particular direction.

This is not a tale of inevitability, any more than the evolution of the lesser spotted woodpecker was inevitable. The very fact that Christianity in eastern Europe inspired different political, social, and intellectual values, and that Christianity in east Asia died out almost entirely is testimony to that. We should not underestimate the potential impact of historical circumstance. Nevertheless, one might conclude that, to borrow Stephen Jay Gould's analog metaphor, were we to re-run the tape of Western history, erasing what actually happened and letting it run again, we might, assuming the same deep Christian conditions and commitments, end up with a set of values that, while superficially different, bore a striking resemblance to those we recognize today.

St. Paul hints at a theological angle on this idea in what we know as his second letter to the church at Corinth. Humans, he tells his readers, are jars of clay—weak, fragile, and often rather chipped and dirty—but they are jars that contain a great treasure that somehow persists and works to the common good, even when we do not. As he puts it elsewhere, "the Spirit helps us in our weakness."

So it is with the influence of Christianity in the West. Christianity, or rather Christians, have been the vessel into which God has poured himself, but they hold that treasure badly: they leak, they spill, they contaminate. And yet, somehow, what they carry persists and preserves and heals and hopes. However many wrong turns Christians take—and the essays in this volume show that Christians have had a profoundly ambiguous relationship with some of the demonstrable human goods we now take for granted—the treasure that they purport to bear remains.

In *A Secular Age*, discussed in chapter 10, Charles Taylor remarks that "our past is sedimented in our present." So it is. The first hope of this book is to draw out some of the ways that our Christian past is sedimented in our increasingly amnesiac present. But the second is to gesture toward how fragments of the good work of God himself remain sedimented in the mess and error and confusion that is ordinary human life.

1

Why the West Is Different

1

History writes historians just as much as historians write history. The presuppositions of an age, the shadows it lives under, the light it thinks it grows toward: all inform how it narrates its past. Hume's histories of England and Gibbon's of Rome could only have been written in the eighteenth century. William Stubbs, Lord Acton, and Jacob Burckhardt all bear the marks of progressive liberty and autonomy that characterize the later nineteenth century. History books may not exemplify their age in the way that styles of architecture are supposed to, but they illustrate them.

So it is today. The secularization thesis ground to a halt at some point in the last quarter of the twentieth century, as the rest of the world veered off Europe's tracks and modernized without losing their religion, and the more muscularly religious emerged from the darkness to batter down the secular defences that the West had erected around itself.

In reaction to this, a number of historians of recent years have been keen to bang the drum for the secular Enlightenment, defining, defending, and celebrating it as the font of all our social and political liberties. These have ranged from the crudest New Atheist caricatures, through Anthony Pagden's *The Enlightenment: And Why it Still Matters*, all the way to Jonathan Israel's awe-inspiring 2,500-page trilogy on the Enlightenment. One should not, of course, expect too much from New Atheist polemics, intended as they are to dish out the most savage punishment beatings to the flimsiest of straw men, but when someone as erudite as Israel writes . . .

Nothing could be more fundamentally mistaken, as well as politically injudicious, than for the European Union to endorse the deeply mistaken notion that "European values" . . . are at least religiously specific and should be recognised as essentially "Christian" values. That the religion of the papacy, Inquisition, and Puritanism should be labelled the quintessence of "Europeanness" would rightly be considered a wholly unacceptable affront by a great majority of thoroughly "European" Europeans.

. . . we clearly have a problem and can be sure that the atmosphere of the age is coloring the pages of our history.

In such a context it takes an impressive and courageous historian to say that in actual fact the Enlightenment is not the source of our political virtues, and that these are better found in distinctly Christian ideas and their institutional setting (whisper it: the Church). Larry Siedentop is that man.

2

Siedentop is an Oxford academic who studied under Isaiah Berlin and whose evident approval of secular liberal values does not mean he is blind to their origins or complacent about their future.

His book *Inventing the Individual* traces the history of certain ideas: that each person exists with worth apart from their social position; that everyone should enjoy equal status under the law; that none should be compelled in their religious beliefs; that each has a conscience that should be respected. These are ideas that many of us deem either obvious or "natural" for humans to hold, or that we locate firmly in the Enlightenment. Such ideas are, in fact, very far from "natural," however, and have their roots many centuries before Voltaire ever put quill to paper.

Inventing the Individual begins in the world of antiquity. This is sometimes taken, in more fanciful quarters, as the nursery of freedom. Yes, slavery might have been institutionalized but polytheism was tolerant, much of it was devoid of serious religion, the free were all equal, and many people even had the vote.

In reality, the ancient world was anything but secular, tolerant, free, or equal. Religion was omnipresent, and the family was everything: the primary social institution and source of identity, the basic unit of social reality, a veritable (and repressive) church in itself. The paterfamilias was effectively a magistrate and high priest with almost unlimited powers. Social roles were fixed and hierarchy and inequality were believed to be built into the universe itself. There was simply no conception of common humanity, and widespread charity (i.e., outside immediate family or clan bonds) "was not deemed a virtue, and would probably have been unintelligible."

This changed with the emergence of city states, which widened the bonds that had been the property of the family, although not by much. Families remained exclusive and powerful, their power now pooled in cities. Citizens belonged to the city and there was little space for individual conscience. The individual simply did not exist outside family, city, or cult.

Cities were inherently religious institutions: quasi-churches, as families had been, patriotism and piety being essentially the same thing. War was tied in with the purpose and worth of the civic realm, and there was no clear distinction between military and economic activity. The pagan gods were no less jealous of their cities than Yahweh was of his people.

As the world changed from city states to empire, these localized social ties loosened but, again, progress was slow. Primogeniture weakened, younger sons became full citizens, the absolute power of the paterfamilias weakened, their sacred status eroded. Such progress was ambiguous, however: local city loyalties (and deities) faded only to be replaced with the God of Rome, whom you crossed at your peril. It was also strictly limited. Women and slaves were still non-persons, confined to the dishonorable and inferior worlds of the home and manual labor. The second-century jurist Gaius could rely on three tests to establish a person's status: Were they free or unfree? A citizen or foreign born? A paterfamilias or in the power of an ancestor? This was enough to tell whether they were worth anything. Roman law, which would play such a significant role in the wake of the Western empire, was limited to relations "between men who shared in the worship of the city, sacrificing at the same altars. They alone were citizens."

There were a few small groups who challenged this social structure, such as the Sophists, peripatetic and paid professional teachers, often of modest backgrounds, who questioned the order of city, empire, and universe. But they were few and limited in their challenge. The powerful idea, favored by some Enlightenment historians and their eager acolytes today, that we can draw any kind of line, let alone a neat and straight one, from the allegedly tolerant and equal liberties of the ancient world to those of today is a myth almost entirely without foundation.

3

It was into this world that Christianity erupted in what Siedentop calls a "moral revolution." Siedentop's description of this eruption is slightly eccentric. He rightly sees the Jewish concept of law—as a statement of God's will that transcends human rational considerations and is thus free from the hierarchical connotations of Roman law—as the foundation for the Christian moral revolution. However, because he deals only briefly with Jewish thought and speaks of intertestamental Judaism as a single thing, he doesn't recognize that, by the time of Jesus, the "wisdom" or Sophia of God is not only spoken of as radiating or emanating from him, but also discernible within creation. In effect, the conception and re-description of divine activity and law in terms that would be comprehensible to the Hellenic mind, had begun before St. Paul.

Similarly, Siedentop locates the Christian moral revolution in Paul rather than Christ (whom he calls "the Christ" throughout) on the somewhat spurious grounds that we can say very little confidently about Jesus' life and teachings. This would be news to many New Testament scholars and, of course, to Paul himself, who had no doubts where his teaching was grounded. Siedentop does not imagine that Paul is an inventor, in the way that some like to claim that Paul "invented" Christianity, but he fails to grant Paul's thought its full intellectual heritage or context. However brilliant and influential he was, Paul was not the sum of early Christianity.

Such quibbles aside, Siedentop is forcefully clear on what Paul's message did revolutionize: "the Christ reveals a God who is potentially present in every believer." Through an act of faith in the Christ, human agency, which is no longer simply a plaything of stars, gods, or fate, can become a medium for God's love. Such an understanding of reality deprived rationality of its aristocratic connotations. Thinking was no longer the privilege of the social elite and became associated not with status but with humility, itself a virtue entirely alien in the ancient world.

Christianity put forward a new idea of a voluntary basis for human association in which people joined together through will and love rather than blood or shared material objectives. In doing so, it helped redefine identity, which was no longer exhausted by social roles, these becoming secondary to the primary relationship with God. For the first time, humans (*all* humans) had a "pre-social" identity, being some*one* before they had some *role*. This provided "an ontological foundation for 'the individual'" through the promise that humans have access to the deepest reality as individuals rather than merely as members of a group. Martyrs in particular became examples of this inner conviction, standing against social and political forces and norms to an extreme degree; examples, if you will, of conscience. "The unintended consequence of the persecution of Christians was to render the idea of the individual, or moral equality, more intelligible."

This was reinforced by the near-universally recognized fact—even among hostile pagans—that churches "amounted to mini-welfare states," tending to treat "our" poor as well as their own, as the emperor Julian the Apostate put it. The Church was inclusive and universal in a way that nothing else was in the ancient world, its sacraments emphasizing the individuality and equality of all.

Even those things, like sexual renunciation, which we modern liberals like to sneer at and are now seen as part of Christianity's repressive side were, in this context, actually liberating. In a society where women were defined by their reproductive role, sexual renunciation was a manifest act of individual will and constituted a powerful statement of independent dignity. Indeed, it was a subtle assertion of control over man—that a woman's body was her own to choose what she did with it rather than simply being a receptacle for a man's desire to breed—an assertion that could only be legitimized by a higher authority. A similar re-balancing of gender power was to be seen in the Church's relentless emphasis that the obligations within marriage were mutual and that male adultery was as worthy of condemnation as female. No one, and certainly not Siedentop, is under any illusion about how church leaders *could* treat women, but in the realm of fundamental ideas there is a different story to be told.

4

What actual impact did this moral reformation have? The answer is a slow one. Siedentop traces the line of Christian ideas through Europe's murkiest centuries.

After the final collapse of the empire in the West in 476, ancient hierarchies were in a shambles. The Church was the last institution left standing and bishops frequently became leading civic figures. They found themselves negotiating with Germanic invaders who had the monopoly of physical force and whose culture entailed the supreme power of the paterfamilias, subordination of women, and inflexible rules concerning inheritance, all of which were antithetical to, or at least in some tension with, core Christian ideas.

The clergy thus often became "diplomats and administrators." Their only viable response to the violence that confronted the broken empire was to wield a moral axe—or, perhaps, moral stick and carrot—with the invaders. On the one hand, they declared that God would judge each and every person for their actions; on the other, they sought to "introduce the norm of 'charity'" into public life. In this way "concern with the fate of the individual soul was nibbling away at a corporate, hierarchical image"—doing unto the Germanic invaders what it had done to the Roman empire they now overran.

Charity was inextricably linked with education and one of the most refreshing critiques in Siedentop's book is of the changing educational landscape of the mid-first millennium. The traditional story here is that ancient learning was free and tolerant, reasonably sophisticated and rational, only to be (brutally) closed down by ignorant monks who, if they thought at all, were obsessed by incomprehensible and essentially meaningless theological details.

While you can certainly defend this line, Siedentop argues persuasively that the educational system of late antiquity was nothing like as polished as we imagine it. The dependence of professors on imperial favor and the strict regulation of students had resulted in forms of intellectual servility and a severely devalued syllabus. Students came from a privileged class and learning was primarily a matter for display, "ornament rather than substance." If you want a more modern comparison, think an Oxford education ca. 1750.

By contrast, Siedentop contends, Christian learning was shaped by the fact that bishops were immersed in the world. They couldn't do rhetoric for rhetoric's sake. Moreover, they were discussing live issues, questions that were not yet settled, unlike most subjects within the lecture halls of late antiquity, and were therefore engaged in thinking rather than just learning. In this way, "the church gave ancient philosophy an 'afterlife,'" as well, of course, as preserving most of ancient texts, Christian and pagan alike, that we have today.

The center for this preservation of thought was the monasteries, but monasteries did more for the idea of the individual than in their educational role alone. Although deplored by many urban clergy at first for their ignorance and cussedness, monks epitomized Christianity's potential for inwardness. They existed alone, defined not by any social role but by God alone. "The monks could be portrayed as a new type of athlete, an athlete who sought not physical perfection or competitive glory but conquest of the will."

When, from the fourth century, they began to live corporately, their "sociability [preserved] the role of individual conscience." The new form of social organization was self-regulatory. Monasteries created "an unprecedented version of authority [where] to be in authority was to be humble." They helped rehabilitate work as a good in itself.

> At the end of antiquity the image [monasticism] offered of a social order founded on equality, limiting the role of force and honouring work, while devoting itself to prayer and acts of charity, gave it a powerful hold over minds.

Again, as with the treatment of women, this is an idealized picture and, again, Siedentop is alert to the monasteries' very many "failings and compromises." But while we dwell in the realm of ideas, it remains an important corrective to the well-worn narratives of monastic darkness, bigotry, and ignorance.

5

Monasticism—at its best—may have preserved and nurtured Christianity's integral values through Europe's most turbulent centuries, but that does not mean the rest of the West was utterly devoid of them. This is the fact that will, perhaps, most surprise the casual reader of *Inventing the Individual*, schooled, as most of us are, in the belief that these were unremittingly barbaric centuries within a generally barbaric millennium.

As an example, Siedentop quotes the remarkable legal formula of King Chilperic, from the mid-sixth century, concerning the status of women in his kingdom.

> A long-standing and wicked custom of our people denies sisters a share with their brothers in their father's land; but I consider this wrong, since my children came equally from God . . . Therefore, my dearest daughter, I hereby make you an equal and legitimate heir with your brothers, my sons.

These are not the words or laws we expect to have emerged from the gloomiest corner of the "Dark Ages."

The surprises do not end with gender. The plight of the poor was repeatedly highlighted in such a way as emphasized the scandal of poverty among those for whom Christ died. "Their sweat and toil made you rich. The rich get their riches because of the poor," thundered Bishop Theodulf of Orleans, like a mitred Marx. "But nature submits you to the same laws. In birth and death you are alike. The same holy water blesses you; you are anointed with the same oils; the flesh and blood of the lamb nourishes you all together."

Slavery remained a live reality in the barbarian kingdoms, the slow direction of travel away from the institution that could be detected in the late antique world being brought to a halt by the fall of the Western empire. Nevertheless, ecclesiastical strictures were introduced to soften the impact. The Visigoths upheld a ban on the capital punishment of slaves by their masters without public trial, and several kingdoms stipulated that married slaves could not be separated, even if they belonged to different masters. This was hardly the Clapham Sect but it nonetheless recognized the humanity of the slave that was a prerequisite for any subsequent abolitionist ventures.

Siedentop makes a great deal of the Carolingian age, which was, in effect, Europe's first mini-Renaissance in the late eighth century. Charlemagne could be heroically brutal, as he showed when he had 4,500 people beheaded outside Bremen in 782. But he also was determined to build a Christian kingdom. Such are the paradoxes of history. There are no straightforward narratives here.

In 792, Europe's greatest ruler wished to secure allegiance of all his people and took oaths of allegiance from every one, including slaves. This, Siedentop rightly points out, would have been unthinkable in antiquity, where one might as well have asked for an oath from a packhorse. Moreover, the oaths were administered in the vernacular so that people could understand them. What mattered was not the public display but the inward consent.

This recognition of inwardness also had a discernible impact on the law. It helped introduce the idea of intentionality into criminal law, judging that what a person intended demanded legal attention alongside what they actually did. This helped replace verdicts that were based on ordeal or combat with those based on evidence. It even raised the idea of conscience in a more abstract sense, as certain prominent clerical advisors, such as Alcuin of York, voiced the belief that enforced belief was a contradiction in terms.

Women's rights, care for the poor, attenuated slavery, legal equality, conscience: none of these was a reality in the period, and it is highly doubtful than any of them were even intended by people at the time. But the seeds that had been promisingly sown by Christianity were not entirely destroyed in the social and political chaos of the early middle ages.

6

The health of the Church took a dive in the centuries following Charlemagne, the papacy becoming a plaything of wealthy Italian families, the disease from the head spreading to the rest of the body, where local landowners regarded parishes as their property, judging and appointing clerics like personal servants, and bishops and abbots lived like local lords. Incumbents were ill-educated, frequently simply family members who purchased or inherited their sinecures.

It was in this context that certain monasteries underwent a slow but immensely important period of reform, seeking the purity and charity that was so evidently missing from the mainstream Church. It was also this context in which the right of the Church to self-govern emerged as an issue that would dominate the next few centuries.

These problems were compacted by growing political instability as the Carolingian empire collapsed, leading to levels of violence not seen since the fifth and sixth centuries. Political chaos bred a mania for castle building in the tenth century and, with it, the emergence of knights, at the time little more than thugs with swords. "Unpunished violence became almost the norm."

The Church tried to bring some peace to the violence but with limited success. In 975, the bishop of Le Puy convened a meeting of knights and peasants of his diocese, eliciting from the former an oath to respect the property of the Church and of paupers and the powerless. Fourteen years later, a church council in Burgundy formally excommunicated those who attacked clerics and "those who stole a beast from the poor or the tillers of soil," stating that pilgrims, women, children, laborers and the instruments of their work, alongside monasteries and cemeteries were to be left "undisturbed and in perpetual peace."

This emphasis on the Peace of God, as it came to be known, made way, in 1017, for the Truce of God movement, an idea—comical to us now, but serious and far from nonsensical at the time—that knights should desist from private warfare from noon Saturday to morning on Monday. This hardly constituted a European-wide amnesty—come Monday morning the bloodshed could begin again—but it attempted to show that continuous warfare was not necessary and that peace was not only possible but morally right. "No Christian should kill another Christian, for whoever kills another Christian undoubtedly sheds the blood of Christ," intoned the Council of Narbonne in 1054. It was such movements and ideas that would develop into a code of conduct between knights, stressing courtesy, honor, and chivalry, a code that might have been marked by a great deal of hypocrisy in the later middle ages, but was certainly better than the unrestrained violence that preceded it.

7

The monastic reformation prepared the way for the papal revolution of the later eleventh century that transformed the European landscape.

In the early years of the new millennium German emperors began to prize the papacy away from Roman families. This, however, opened the way for the more intransigent, monastic attitudes of Cluny, the chief reformed monastery, to get into Rome, and thereafter an epic struggle with the Holy Roman Empire.

In its desire to reform and clean out its own house, the papacy sought self-discipline and developed an impressive and newly consolidated body of law. The idea of papal rule, long an ambition, became a reality, one that was embedded in universal and (subversively egalitarian) law. Monk-popes gave way to legal ones. General councils and papal decrees, legates and correspondence multiplied. The first universities—Bologna, Paris, Montpellier, Oxford—were founded, primarily in order to promote the study of law. Gratian composed his enormously influential *Decretum*, a textbook systematization of canon law.

Europe developed a coherent body of law for the first time since the days of the Roman empire, although this time the presuppositions on which the law was built were crucially different. In Siedentop's words, "by identifying natural law with biblical revelation and Christian morality, Gratian gave it an egalitarian bias—and a subversive potential—utterly foreign to the ancient world's understanding of natural law as 'everything in its right place.'" The result was that "the standards introduced into social life by canon law were more humane and equitable than those that had preceded them." To take one example: the Fourth Lateran Council, held in 1215, effectively abolished trial by ordeal by forbidding clergy to take part in it. In its place, new ideas of punishment, separate from retaliation or retribution, were developed, alongside a growing emphasis on confession, penance, and deterrence.

Law also had a critical importance in the formation of towns. "Canonists promoted an understanding of the corporation as a voluntary association of individuals who remain the source of its authority, rather than as a body constituted by superior authority and wholly dependent on that authority for its identity." This was of incalculable importance in fostering an emerging sense of fraternal responsibility and freedom among guilds and, through them, the towns that were emerging in the conditions of greater peace following the millennium. Unlike towns and cities in the ancient—and in the

Islamic—world, which were never legally constituted or founded as autonomous legal entities, the Western European town had its own independent corporate existence, legitimacy, and often structure of self-governance, all of which were reflected in the development of the town charter.

So it was that by around 1200, Western Europe had legal and moral structures in place that marked the continent out from the rest of the world. There was, in the papacy, an independent self-governing institution where, in theory, "secular" power did not extend. There was a concept of political authority that, while treated as coming from of God, was not divine in itself: sacred but also desacralized. There was the conviction that divinely authorized moral authority, in which—in theory at least—all people were equal and equally under judgement, extended over everyone. There was, in guilds and towns, the emergence of a legally secured sphere of what would one day be called civil society. There was a centralized and systematized structure of law. There were even ideas of a "social contract" kind, whereby scholars like Manegold of Lautenbach argued that the authority of the king was conditional. The combination was potent and unprecedented.

8

There was one further development in the Western concept of political authority generated, albeit accidentally, by the papacy in the high middle ages, which was to prove essential.

Canon lawyers had long grappled with the idea of what constituted legitimate authority, a far from theoretical question when so very much authority was invested in one man. Papal claims to moral and political supremacy reached their apogee around 1300, by which time they were—ironically—blurring the "secular" separation of Church and "state" that the papacy itself had created. What—heaven forfend!—would happen if Christendom were to find itself with a heretical pope sitting in Rome?

At one level, the answer was obvious. God's law stood over the pope just as much as it did any king or commoner. But that answer only got you so far. How would you *know* that the pope erred? Who was to judge? And, even more problematically, who was to do anything about it? The answer to these troubling questions that theologians and lawyers edged toward was, in effect, to locate authority not in the head of the institution but throughout its body.

This became a painfully live issue with the Great Schism at the end of the fourteenth century, when cardinals turned against the recently elected Pope Urban VI and anti-pope Clement VII, who had strong French support. It was then made even worse when the choice of a supposedly compromise candidate, Alexander V, in 1409, proved unacceptable and Christendom was left with not two but three popes.

This scandal was eventually negotiated, by means of various councils, but the immediate legacy it left was to elevate the power of the council over that of the pope or, in more secular terms, of the electors over the elected. Moreover, the model was approved by secular rulers who had long envied and sought to imitate the Church's sophisticated, self-regulating, centralized authoritarian structure, but at the same time resented its interventionist role within their territories. For kings, seeking to give their authority a more secure, territorial basis and to minimize papal interference, the lessons of the Great Schism and the Conciliar movement were instructive and invaluable. The Church's ideas were thus, eventually, deployed against it, its powers reduced by "liberal" political commitments it had generated.

9

In one sense the story ends here. In Siedentop's words,

> The roots of liberalism were firmly established in the arguments of philosophers and canon lawyers by the fourteenth and early fifteenth centuries: belief in a fundamental equality of status as the proper basis for a legal system; belief that enforcing moral conduct is a contradiction in terms; a defence of individual liberty, through the assertion of fundamental or "natural" rights; and, finally, the conclusion that only a representative form of government is appropriate for a society resting on the assumption of moral equality.

Of course, it doesn't. Indeed, the tragedy is that from such promising trajectory, the narrative takes a discernible dive.

The future was promising. The movement set in train by papacy and canonists blossomed into the nominalism of the fourteenth century, when an even more radical emphasis on natural rights and personal autonomy emerged, particularly in the thought of William of Ockham, whom Siedentop discusses at some length.

It was just at this point, however, that the historical vehicle on which these ideas were travelling took a sharp handbrake turn. The successful resolution of the Great Schism helped establish a newly confident papacy, which then ignored the conciliar reforms that had re-established it. At the same time, increasingly assertive national kingdoms began to claw back power from the papacy, which became still more absolutist and brittle. The cause of reform stalled in the later fifteenth century, creating tensions that exploded in the sixteenth.

At first, the Reformers set the cause of political liberty back centuries in their unquestioning elevation of secular authority. It is telling that in the later sixteenth century, when Protestant leaders found themselves needing to formulate arguments against political powers that turned out not to be as Reformed as they had hoped, they often, quietly and shamefacedly, had to appeal to Catholic political thought for their raw materials. More damagingly, different Christian factions attempted to restore or reform Christendom by an appeal to force. As Siedentop says, "increasingly, the adjective 'barbarous'—which in earlier centuries had been applied . . . to the beliefs and practices of the tribes overrunning the Western Roman empire—would be reapplied to the attitudes and actions of the churches."

The Church, having led the way—in ideas if not always in practice—toward equality, freedom, conscience, and restrained and judged authority, became the object that was casting a shadow over these political virtues, one that many came to believe needed to be toppled in order to secure them.

10

Counterfactuals may be fun but they are futile. "If the reform undertaken by the councils had been well carried out, the Reformation might have been prevented," once remarked the nineteenth-century French historian François Guizot, one of Siedentop's guiding lights. It's one of history's biggest ifs.

Whatever might have happened, the Renaissance began a reassessment of the classical past. It was, in many ways, a partial and problematic reassessment. "Italian humanists drew on the ancient world as a kind of quarry, without asking too much about its original structure." Be that as it may, it gained its own momentum. The Enlightenment adopted the narrative, adding a strident anticlericalism that had originally been absent, and the history of Europe, in particular its political progress, was changed. Between the Renaissance itself and the nineteenth-century historians who first named and defined it, the story of how Christianity crafted the building blocks that made the West was lost.

Siedentop is not the first to rediscover it. Indeed, in rarefied academic circles the works of people like Brian Tierney and Harold Berman on the role of the canonists and conciliarists has long been known and highly respected. Siedentop draws on them and other sources to bring the tale to a wider audience that is, it seems, largely ignorant of the deep reasons why the West became what it did.

2

Religiously Secular:
The Making of America

————•◦•————

1

The theologian Benjamin Warfield once remarked that the Reformation could profitably be understood as a battle within the theology of St. Augustine, specifically between Augustine's doctrine of grace and his doctrine of the Church. It is a pleasing formulation and one that might, mutatis mutandis, be appropriated to explain the genesis of America. If the Reformation was an argument forged within the pages of Augustine, so the United States emerged from the pages of the Bible, the result of a clash between the doctrine of holiness and the doctrine of freedom.

Given the United States' quintessential modernity, its roots in Enlightenment thought, the alleged "secularism" of its polity, and the apparent indifference, even impiety, of some of its more prominent Founding Fathers, the idea that America is the result of a battle within Christian theology might seem somewhat far-fetched. Yet any "secular" reading of American history is to mistake the waves for the currents. Much of the surface spectacle of the epochal event was, apparently, non-religious—although, we shall see, not as much as is sometimes thought. But it was the formidable deep-sea currents of Christian thought that helped shape those waves and thereby the contours of the new nation.

2

The surface spectacle of the Revolution was indeed seemingly non-religious, even irreligious. Thomas Paine, sometimes called the Father of the American Revolution, was as scornful of Christian doctrine as it was possible to be (outside France) at the end of the eighteenth century, as fierce in his deism as he was contemptuous of revealed religion and clericalism. Thomas Jefferson was hardly less anticlerical and widely smeared as an outright atheist in his tumultuous 1800 presidential campaign. Benjamin Franklin became a deist when young (ironically after reading Robert Boyle's refutation of deism) and only rarely attended religious services. There is clearly much secular hay to be made here.

Beyond such heterodox pyrotechnics, the Enlightenment traditions of natural rights (albeit filtered through the Christian John Locke) and radical Whig republicanism were highly significant in grounding the ideas and framing the objectives of the revolutionaries. Even among the more obviously pious Founding Fathers, historians have detected a telling absence of biblical and theological arguments. "Despite the centrality of the Bible in early American culture, the founding generation rejected or deemphasized the Bible and biblical rhetoric," wrote Wilson Carey McWilliams in his essay "The Bible in the American Political Tradition." Many believers accused the framers of the Constitution of selling out the nation's Christianity and showing "cold indifference towards religion": "if civil rulers won't acknowledge God, he won't acknowledge them; and they must perish from the way." As John Fea wrote in his book *Was America Founded as a Christian Nation?*, "when one examines the specific arguments made by colonial political leaders in the years leading up to 1776, one is hard pressed to find any Christian or biblical language apart from a few passing references to God."

For all that this view still garners support, recent historical scholarship—in particular work by Mark Noll and Daniel Dreisbach—has drawn attention to the biblical and theological outlook that was, in fact, hidden in plain sight. Six years ago, I began a book entitled *Freedom and Order: History, Politics and the English Bible* by claiming that the Bible had been the single most influential text in English, latterly British, political history, a brazen claim in a British context that turns an ever-blinder eye to its Christian roots. Precisely the same case could be made for America. Indeed, this is more or less exactly what Mark Noll does in his book *In the Beginning Was the Word*, claiming that "it is no exaggeration to claim that the Bible has been—and by far—the single most widely read text, distributed object, and referenced book in all of American history," into which we might slip the adjective "political."

The first complete book printed in America was the Bay Psalm book, originating in Cambridge, Massachusetts, in 1640. Of the 25,000 or so separate items published over the next century and a half (as identified by the North American Imprints Program of the American Antiquarian Society), the second largest proportion (after the 28 percent printed for colonial government) were religious: 16 percent comprising sermons, prayer books, hymnals, and psalmbooks. Religious books also had far larger print runs, the only publications with larger ones being almanacs (which were hardly devoid of biblical information themselves).

The fact that 53 percent of these publications originated in New England, and indeed 37 percent from Massachusetts alone, helps explain this biblical preponderance. This wasn't solely a New England phenomenon, however, especially after the First Great Awakening of the 1730s and '40s. Hunger for the text rose in the wake of the revival, and the latter half of the century was, if anything, more biblicist than the first half, in spite of the slow penetration of deistic and radical thought. Contrary to some of the assertions outlined above, and as discussed in a later chapter, the Revolution was awash with biblical rhetoric. The very fact that Paine himself made repeated use of the Scriptures, in spite of his growing contempt for revealed religion, testifies to the omnipresence and significance of the Bible. He may not have meant it, but he knew he had to talk about it to persuade his audience.

Moreover, the biblical register only grew after the Revolution with the impact of the Second Great Awakening. "The Old Testament is truly so omnipresent in the American culture of 1800 or 1820 that historians have as much difficulty taking cognizance of it as of the air people breathed," wrote Perry Miller in his 1955 essay "The Garden of Eden and the Deacon's Meadow." The Bible was the intellectual medium of the age.

3

In one regard, "medium" is the wrong metaphor to use here, as the Bible—or at least biblical reflection—was not one single uniform homogenous entity in which all Americans lived and moved and had their being. Less the climate of the American mind, it was more like its weather: a vast, complex, varied, and seemingly contradictory set of ideas and commitments under which all Americans lived.

That weather had turned violent in sixteenth- and seventeenth-century Europe, driving many early settlers westward. They went in search of freedom and of holiness. The first of these is (allegedly) self-evident for us moderns; our entire political, social, and economic outlook is predicated on a certain understanding of and commitment to freedom. The second is more complex, not least, as Jonathan Haidt indicates in his book *The Righteous Mind: Why Good People Are Divided by Religion and Politics*, because so many "WEIRDs"—Western, Educated, Industrialized, Rich, and Democratic moderns—seem to lack any "taste buds" for the holy or sacred. Haidt's formulation of sanctity—that it pertains to senses of disgust, taboo, contamination, disease, and their opposites, which have been prevalent and seemingly innate throughout most of human history—is helpful, especially when he allies it to another "taste bud," that of authority, that many WEIRDs also lack. However it is understood and articulated for a contemporary audience, the Anglophone search for holiness—for lives and communities of moral purity, uncontaminated by the wickedness and worldliness that surrounded them—was central to the early American project.

Critically, that dream of holiness could take many different forms. The most familiar of these is visible in the history of New England. Seeking to complete the work of the Reformation and found a society of saints, a New Israel, an exemplary city on a hill, "Puritans" sailed into the unknown and founded their fledgling societies on resolutely biblical grounds, seeking what biblical Israel and contemporary Europe so singularly lacked.

Early legal codes, such as that adopted by John Davenport's New Haven Colony in the late 1630s, relied heavily on the Torah as their model and template. Economic questions, political arrangements, social life, as well, of course, as personal morality, were all decided by reference to the Bible. Violating biblical prohibitions against profiteering or price gouging warranted not only censure by the church but also punishment by the courts. Families would live, merchants would trade, and authorities would govern according to the Scriptures. This was a holy society.

Although the best known, this was not the only vision of holiness that settlers drew from the pages of the Bible. Indeed, in their own way, those colonies marked by their loyalty to the ecclesiastical and political authorities in England, rather than by any Puritan autonomy or congregationalism, were as determined to build holy societies as those in search of the New Jerusalem. Thus the law codes of early Virginia, for example, showed as much deference to the Bible as those of New England, requiring that "no man shall speak any word, or do any act, which may tend to the derision, or despite of God's holy word upon pain of death." These settlers carried with them the deep-rooted assumption of European Christendom, preserved on both major sides of the continent's increasingly bitter divide, namely that a stable kingdom needed religious unity. In the words of James Hutson, the chief of the Manuscripts Division at the Library of Congress, "Anything short of a national uniformity in religion, the ministers claimed would bring 'divers mischiefs upon the Commonwealth.'"

Such states sought to maintain confessional unity and loyalty and to encourage public virtue in order to remain secure. The refrain from Isaiah 49:23—"kings shall be thy nursing fathers, and their queens thy nursing mothers" (KJV)—was repeatedly cited as the biblical justification for divinely sanctioned interventionist royal authority. Settlements such as those that took root in Virginia might not have been pursuing a new Jerusalem, but that did not mean holiness, and the social order it brought, was any less important to them. A holy society could be an ordered and established society too.

The pursuit of societal holiness faded in the second half of the seventeenth century. In New England, it lost its prophetic, millennial edge. According to Mark Noll, "for the first generation, religion acted directly to chastise merchants for sins of avarice; for the second and third generations, religion continued to caution merchants about economic excess . . . for the fourth generation, religion declared that the market practices of an integrated 'empire of goods' were ordained by God as part of his creation of the world."

This prophetic blunting was then redirected by the Great Awakening in the second quarter of the eighteenth century. This placed a powerful emphasis on personal holiness without, at the same time, translating that into a societal vision. The colonies did not return to the early vision in which all forms of political, legal, and economic life could be directed by recourse to the Scriptures. Gone were attempts to build the New Jerusalem. In its place was the vision of a universal priesthood of believers whose familiarity with the Scriptures enabled, indeed, commanded, them to live holy lives.

This, however, brought its own problems, as a universal priesthood of believers gave fuel for uncontrolled enthusiasm and theological hubris that could alienate other believers, fracture fellowships, divide churches, and scandalize the authorities. Personal visions of holiness, it transpired, were no more concordant than societal visions. Sanctified believers could break up just as easily as sanctified societies and both, of course, rubbed uneasily against the more authoritarian vision of holiness that persisted in American culture.

In the half century following the Glorious Revolution of 1688, this vision only grew as colonial America became more self-consciously British, its loyalty to monarchy strengthening, even as royal officials paid it little attention. The Colonies faced near-constant military threats from France or French-backed Catholic powers and repeatedly engaged in major conflicts. King William's War of 1688–97 corresponded to the Nine Years War (or the War of League of Augsburg), Queen Anne's War of 1702–13 to the War of Spanish Succession, and King George's War of 1744–48 to the War of Austrian Succession. The royal names of these conflicts imply a certain distance from the governing homeland, but the causes into which the Colonies were drawn were shared ones. Accordingly, the same potent mix of Protestantism, liberty, and prosperity that characterized eighteenth-century Britain was evident in America, as was the instrumental nature of popular piety. The long-standing identification of holiness with socio-political order placed ever greater emphasis on the latter, "the true end for which religion is established," in William Warburton's famous formulation from his *Alliance between Church and State,* being "not to provide for the true faith but for civil utility." The enthusiasm, often bordering on hysteria, of the First Great Awakening simply reinforced the point. America needed holiness but the right kind of holiness: "godly, righteous and sober," to use the words of the

Prayer Book, and not godly, self-righteous, and, frankly, spiritually inebriated.

4

If holiness was the vision that drew settlers westward in the early seventeenth century, freedom was the means many felt was necessary to achieving it. For Anglican Americans, particularly during the Anglicizing decades of the early eighteenth century, holiness demanded order. For those of a more Puritan disposition, it required freedom, and they could point to the Bible to prove it.

The Scriptures spoke of freedom almost as much as they did holiness, placing it in stark opposition to the slavery that was fundamental and omnipresent in society. The Exodus was, naturally, a foundation stone. Jesus' self-proclaimed mission was "to set at liberty them that are bruised" (according to the King James translation of Luke 4:18). St. Paul spoke of "the glorious liberty of the children of God" (Rom. 8:21), and how where "the Spirit of the Lord is, there is liberty" (2 Cor. 3:17), and of "the liberty wherewith Christ hath made us free" (Gal. 5:1).

The motif was central, or at least became central, to the Reformed tradition. Having loaded the magistrate with unwarranted hopes in the earliest decades of the Reformation, and then finding themselves woefully disappointed, disillusioned, and afraid for the future of their movement, Protestants hastily developed arguments for freedom of conscience and political liberty (often, ironically, quietly borrowing rather more sophisticated Catholic arguments). Numerous publications, such as the influential *Vindiciae, Contra Tyrannos*, published pseudonymously in 1579, set out the justification for resistance to, and rebellion against, tyrannical rulers and deployed arguments that would become mainstream in the seventeenth century and, in turn, in pre-Revolutionary America.

Several generations later, chapter 20 of the Westminster Confession of 1646, "Of Christian Liberty, and Liberty of Conscience," proclaimed how "the liberty which Christ has purchased for believers under the Gospel consists in their freedom from the guilt of sin, and condemning wrath of God, the curse of the moral law." This liberty was "not intended by God to destroy, but mutually to uphold and preserve one another," a sentiment that echoed Paul's advice in Galatians 5:13 that believers should "only use not liberty for an occasion to the flesh, but by love serve one another." However, the confession also went on to state boldly that "God alone is Lord of the conscience, and has left it free from the doctrines and commandments of men." The gospel of freedom was no superficially spiritual affair. It meant freedom down to the deepest levels of worship, behavior, and conscience.

Discomfortingly, however, newly founded Puritan settlements found themselves as the authorities in their new Israel, and they discovered, almost as rapidly as Luther had done in the 1520s, that people would often use their newly found freedom in the wrong way. Separatist colonists found themselves having to deal with intensely devout but troublesome figures like Roger Williams and Anne Hutchinson, who rejected attempts to impose holiness on them and made the same appeal to freedom as they themselves had made in England. Inevitably, persecution accompanied persecuted Puritans across the Atlantic like rats in their ships. The cause of freedom could never be taken for granted.

Moreover, while the vision of Christian liberty was palpably tarnished in England by the events of 1640–60, giving way to a confident reestablishment of ecclesiastical authority at the Restoration, the Colonies, spared the violence of the English civil wars and the worst excesses of the Commonwealth, didn't lose the vision in the same way. Eighty years later, the Great Awakening boosted not only the Colonies' biblicism but also the doctrine of Bible-as-freedom, the powerful inspiration and manifestation of God's spirit in individual believers serving to act as a kind of acid against any structures of holiness, especially Christendom-flavored ones. In Mark Noll's apt words, "revival pushed colonial regimes with established churches toward a fork in the road: either abandon the inherited structures of Christendom in order to enjoy personal experience of divine grace, or resist claims concerning that personal manifestation in order to preserve a unified, sanctified society. In all colonial regions, the revivals built momentum for choosing against Christendom."

All these factors—the long-standing Protestant commitment to freedom of worship and conscience, the recognition that such freedom always needed to be defended, the absence of any post-Interregnum backlash against liberty, and the impact of the Great Awakening—meant that the idea of Bible-as-freedom was a deep and powerful current in the run up to the War of Independence.

5

Inevitably, the doctrines of holiness and freedom—both equally and thoroughly grounded in the pages of Scripture—came into collision with one another.

The latter had its cracks. Whose freedom, and how much freedom, and who was to adjudicate the limits of that freedom were questions not easily answered. The doctrine of holiness had more, however. No matter that each group drew its inspiration from the same Bible; the Puritan settlers of New England, the establishment clerics of Virginia, and the reborn believers of the First Great Awakening each had importantly different understandings of holiness, or at least of how it should be manifested.

This—plus a good helping of circumstance and pragmatism—was the reason why the thirteen states had such a patchwork of church-state relations on the eve of, and for some years after, the Revolution. American "secularism," as we might now anachronistically introduce the term, was born of this clash of Christian freedom and Christian holiness, rather than being the result of any worked-out secular "world view." If the US was born a "secular" nation, it was for profoundly Christian reasons. It was, so to speak, religiously secular.

This was the reason why, on the eve of the Revolution, there was no straightforward, let alone universal, desire to separate church and state for reasons of alleged public neutrality. Indeed, James Hutson has remarked how he was unable to find "a scintilla of evidence . . . there was a popular groundswell for the separation of church and state," not only before but even in the years immediately after independence.

Instead, there was a rich, messy patchwork of different, deeply felt, and deeply rooted theological commitments pertaining to the proper balance between holiness and freedom in a society and its polity. Some states enforced holiness with vigor. Virginia established a representative assembly with control of its religious affairs within a decade of the colony's foundation in 1607. In 1643, its new royalist governor declared his intention to preserve "the purity and doctrine and unity of the church" and sought to expel Puritans and Catholics. The colony enthusiastically passed an Act for Suppressing Quakers in 1659 and an Act of Conformity in 1662. Not much changed over the ensuing century. By the time of the Revolution the colony was, in Hutson's words, "an ecclesiastical dinosaur," an Anglican monolith proud of its coercive uniformity and happy to boast about its true and pure religion, albeit of a notably low-church variety. This was a colony still informed by, indeed fixated on, one particular conceptualization of holiness, at the expense of others and, of course, at the expense of the doctrine of freedom.

Massachusetts Bay Colony adopted a similar approach but with less success. The colony's charter, issued by Charles I, permitted the governor and company to:

> establish all Manner of ... Lawes [and] Statutes ... for the directing, [and] ruling ... whereby our said People ... may be so religiously, peaceable, and civilly governed, as their good Life and orderly Conversation, may win and incite the Natives of Country, to the Knowledge and Obedience of the only true God and Saviour of Mankind, and the Christian Faith.

This was an edict for government-directed holiness, and the Massachusetts Bay Colony took its responsibilities seriously; it threatened, arrested, or expelled many shades of religious opinion between 1630 and 1660 as well as hanging a few Quakers for sedition. The problem was, however, that even by the time it was founded in 1628, the colony had incorporated a significant number of Puritans who had been settling in Plymouth from 1620 and had reached about 20,000 by mid-century. Enforced holiness (of any flavor) became difficult to sustain in these circumstances (in spite of the colony's best efforts) and the authorities' efforts to do so weakened in the last third of the century. The new Royal Charter of 1691 stipulated "liberty of Conscience allowed in the Worship of God," despite the fact that the Congregational Church remained established, with an attendant right to taxation.

Other states found themselves adopting a similar approach through a similar mix of pragmatism and principle. Maryland was unusual from the beginning in being founded by the Catholic George Calvert, who sought to make the state a refuge for persecuted English Catholics.

Accordingly, Maryland attracted a comparably large number of Catholic settlers, making a Massachusetts Bay-style established holiness impracticable from the start, not to mention against its founders' principles. Such mutual forbearance didn't survive the Interregnum, in which Maryland Protestants attacked and expelled Catholics, but the pendulum swung again with the Restoration and then once more, albeit less violently, with the newly assertive royal government in the 1690s. Eventually, despite this royalist turn, the state's coercive holiness was watered down in the 1700s to encompass both Anglican establishment and (some) freedom of conscience, a settlement not so far from Massachusetts, although arrived at by different means.

In contrast to those states like Virginia in which established holiness remained supreme, and those like Maryland and Massachusetts that tempered their coercive holiness with measures of freedom, some appeared to favor a vision of freedom, albeit one tempered with holiness. And although pragmatism was never irrelevant in this matter, reasons of principle were often foundational.

Rhode Island was founded by Roger Williams in 1636 after his expulsion from Massachusetts Bay Colony for religious nonconformity. The result was a principled adherence to freedom over coerced holiness, although one that was somewhat strengthened by the growing recognition that religious toleration was good for the economy (something that helped to explain one of the great geopolitical puzzles of the age, namely how the tiny Dutch republic had become a major global power). Bible-as-freedom had few challenges in Rhode Island, which might help explain why the state was the first colony to renounce its allegiance to the British crown in 1776.

New York State's appropriation from the Dutch in 1664 meant that establishment holiness was always going to be difficult, and when its authorities recognized the commercial benefit of toleration and liberty of conscience prototyped by the Dutch, it became undesirable too. The state's de facto denominational pluralism overwhelmed periodic attempts to set up an Anglican establishment, and even though the Church of England was established in 1693, its establishment was weak, disputed, and widely resented. Freedom triumphed, although this time more by accident than theological design.

The best-known principled assertion of religious freedom was to be seen in Pennsylvania. Like New York State, Pennsylvania was founded and settled by the Dutch half a century before it came into English possession, and so it had already developed a de facto religious pluralism. No less importantly, however, Charles II granted a land charter to the Quaker William Penn in 1681, and Penn turned the colony into a beacon of freedom of conscience. Although not entirely devoid of the signs of established holiness—Sabbath laws remained, as did penalties for those speaking "loosely or profanely" about God—and not immune to pragmatic arguments—Penn also believed that toleration was a stimulant to economic growth—Pennsylvania stood as the best icon of Bible-as-freedom in the colonies.

There was a clear direction of travel among the thirteen states in pre-Revolutionary America. Every colony established after 1642 had some measure of toleration built into its governing structures, most having some de facto religious pluralism already entrenched. For all that the half century after the Glorious Revolution saw a reassertion of English, and Anglican, identity, loyalty, and organization, efforts to legislate for earlier visions of holiness were few and generally failed.

The drift from holiness to freedom was, however, to a freedom firmly grounded in, and in most cases justified by, Christian commitments. Reading later secular understandings of freedom into colonial laws is a serious anachronism. Maryland's 1649 Act Concerning Religion, for example, might have promised "free exercise" of religion, using the exact words of the First Amendment nearly a century and a half later, but it also authorized the state to hang non-Trinitarian Christians. Colonial freedom was religious freedom, for better and for worse.

6

So it is that the political world in which the Founding Fathers found themselves was not only biblical, but awash with theological convictions about the proper function of the state, in particular whether the state should enforce (some kind of) holiness or whether, for no less biblical reasons, it should seek to secure freedom of worship and even (a measure of) freedom of conscience.

The general move was clearly from the former toward the latter over the century and a half of the colonies' existence, a move that liberally mixed principle and theological arguments with personal experiences and practical considerations such as de facto religious pluralism and the economic incentive exemplified by the Dutch. The matter was anything but settled by the 1770s, however, with a range of "settlements" that encompassed more or less the entire spectrum from Virginian "holiness" to Pennsylvanian "freedom."

A neat example of these tensions can be glimpsed in the convening of the First Continental Congress in Philadelphia on September 5, 1774. The following day Thomas Cushing of Massachusetts proposed the proceedings should begin with a prayer. The suggestion was controversial, although not because it was transgressing secular norms or breaching some proto Wall of Separation, as might be the case today. The prayer was an issue not because it shouldn't be said but because there were so many ways, reflecting so many different theological traditions, that it should. The problem was not a would-be naked public square but one that had too many garments from which to choose. In the words of John Adams, "we were so divided in religious sentiments, some Episcopalians, some Quakers, some Anabaptists, some Presbyterians and some Congregationalists . . . that we could not join in the same Act of Worship." (The final irony in this story is that the man who was chosen as a satisfactory compromise candidate to deliver the prayer and then to minister as chaplain to Congress, the Anglican Jacob Duche, defected to the British three years later.)

Thereafter, Congress showed innumerable signs of its religiosity. That year it declared that July 20 should be the first national day of "public humiliation, fasting and prayer." Thereafter, it issued a fast day proclamation every March and a thanksgiving proclamation every October. As Daniel Dreisbach notes, it "adopted and preached to the American people the political theology of the national covenant." It did everything in its power to create a pious military, irreligion in the ranks being a particular nightmare of governing authorities. It was determined to maintain the supply of Bibles that had been interrupted by hostilities, eventually commissioning a new publication. Secularism, in its modern conceptualization, was simply not in the cards.

What was the decisive turn in the tussle between biblically grounded political-secured holiness and freedom? As a later chapter discusses, the Scriptures were adopted by both sides in the War of Independence, albeit more imaginatively, vividly, and successfully by the revolutionaries. However else the debate about biblically justified political tyranny and liberty, loyalty, or rebellion worked out, though, what was beyond doubt—at least in the revolutionaries' minds—was that the British were on the side of coerced and established holiness. No matter how much various states wished to justify their legislated holiness, that model had become irredeemably tainted by the war. The balance had been tipped, irrevocably, to freedom.

Change was nonetheless slow. Seven of the fourteen states that comprised the union in 1791 authorized some form of establishment of religion by law. The historian John Witte has compiled a remarkably long list of "friendly aids" and special recognition that national and state governments offered to the churches in the half century following independence, including publicly endorsing Christian practices, rituals, and prayers; sponsoring or underwriting chaplains and missionaries; offering property grants, tax subsidies, and tax exemptions; and using Christian marks and verses on currency, stamps, seals, state documents, courthouse walls, schools, public buildings, and beyond. The last state to disestablish its church, Massachusetts, did so only in 1833.

No less noteworthy is the fact that the onward march of freedom over holiness was powered not by American proto-secularists, of whom there were precious few, but by the new wave of believers. In Hutson's words, "by producing legions of Baptists and Methodists who were opposed in principle to tax support of religion and who, in addition, were generally 'common men,' suspicious of religious elites, the Second Great Awakening put the remnant of religious establishment in New England—the support of ministers and churches by taxation—on the path to extinction." The vision of freedom had decisively defeated that of holiness. The result was a form of what we now call secularism, but it was a secularism conceived, born, nurtured, and released upon the world by means of deep-rooted Christian ideas and commitments.

3

Trouble with the Law: Magna Carta and the Limits of the Law

—•◦•—

1

The praise with which we shower Magna Carta can get a bit embarrassing. The Great Charter is, according to Barack Obama, the document that "first laid out the liberties of man." It is the reason, according to David Cameron's 2014 Party Conference speech, why we do not need lecturing on human rights from judges in Strasbourg. It has been heralded as the foundation of good government, of democracy, of the United States Declaration of Independence, and of the Universal Declaration of Human Rights. If you have read Sellar and Yeatman's spoof, *1066 and All That,* you may remember that it was rather well described as "the chief cause of Democracy in England, and thus a Good Thing for everyone (except the Common People)." But it was surely best celebrated by the comedian Tony Hancock, orating before his fellow jurymen and women in the episode of the BBC radio and television series *Hancock's Half Hour* called "Twelve Angry Men," when he asked rhetorically "Does Magna Carta mean nothing to you? Did she die in vain?"

The document itself can be a bit perplexing when you first read it. It is sometimes remarked that when undergraduates first open a copy of *The Origin of Species* they expect to find a text that vigorously shakes the intellectual foundations of European civilization to the core, and are therefore surprised and disappointed to find themselves reading page after page about pigeons. So it is for those who first encounter Magna Carta. We expect a magnificent declaration concerning human dignity and freedom but are surprised to find a range of technical and obscure royal concessions covering everything from tax and inheritance to forestry practice and the location of fish weirs.

Moreover, while most people know that the document was a product of highly specific and contingent circumstances (essentially King John's military disasters and endless need for money), fewer know that in the first instance it was a complete failure. Not only did King John tear it up—metaphorically speaking—as soon as he had the chance but, as the medieval historian J. C. Holt once observed:

> It was intended as a peace and provoked war. It pretended to state customary law and it promoted disagreement and contention. It was legally valid for no more than three months, and even within that period its terms were never properly executed.

All of which invites the question: Is it all myth? Is Magna Carta a legend, in the fantastical sense of that word? Have the British, and even more the Americans, been celebrating in 2015 without good cause?

The answer is "no." It is in Magna Carta that we first see, enshrined in law, the demand for due process within the judicial system. It is in Magna Carta that we first see limitations placed on the monarch as someone answerable to the law. And it is in Magna Carta that we first see rights language extended to "all free men," rather than restricted to an elite group. There is something to celebrate here, but in celebrating we should neither sacralize nor desecrate.

2

The basic story of Magna Carta is still reasonably well known. King John acceded to the throne in 1199. He was, by all accounts, a dreadful man and a dreadful monarch. His need for money was insatiable, motivated largely by his desire to maintain, and then to recapture, his lands in Normandy. His means for raising it was brutal and arbitrary, and showed precious little regard for due process, custom, or basic principles of fairness.

John's big campaign to recapture the land was comprehensively crushed in 1214, and when he returned home he was humiliated and impoverished and politically weak enough to be forced to negotiate in London with his furious barons. The negotiations were inconclusive. John wriggled. The barons fumed. And eventually, on May 5, 1215, they renounced their fealty to the king, which was effectively a declaration of war.

In reality, neither the barons nor King John wanted outright hostilities. Full-scale civil war had brutalized the country for two decades in the previous century and no one was keen to return to it. Nevertheless, the conflict was real and on the morning of Sunday, May 17, the barons and their associates seized London and replaced the mayor with one of their own men. This forced the king's hand and a truce was hastily arranged. After much back and forth, the king and the barons assembled on the fields of Runnymede, close to both the king's base at Windsor Castle and the barons' base at Staines.

The precise details of what led up to the drafting and then the sealing of Magna Carta are far from clear. Whatever exactly happened, what was then known only as "The Charter of Runnymede" was sealed by a reluctant monarch on June 15. Peace was duly declared, London returned, and the barons renewed their pledge of fealty to the king. And that was that. A combination of selfishness, intransigence, and expediency lay behind this most totemic of legal documents.

3

Now, none of this of course means the document was simply *selfish* or expedient. There are certainly many highly specific clauses in it. Many of them address the king's immediate financial dealings—or rather misdealings—and place restrictions on his ability to extract money through inheritance relief (Clauses 2 and 3) and the remarriage of widows (Clause 7), preventing him from unjustly seizing the land of a debtor (Clause 9), and severely limiting the situations in which the king could levy tax without "the general consent of the realm" (Clauses 12 and 15). Other clauses, however, move away from the immediate to the more principled. Three principles in particular are worth noting.

The first principle is that of "due process"—emphasizing the importance of following legal processes and of operating within a legal framework. This is referred to in a number of clauses but most famously in Clause 39, which reads:

> No free man shall be seized or imprisoned, or stripped of his rights or possessions, or outlawed or exiled, or deprived of his standing in any way, nor will we proceed with force against him, or send others to do so, except by the lawful judgment of his peers or by the law of the land.

This is, of course, highly specific to the circumstances but it is also principled.

The second principle that occurs within the charter is that concerning the arbitration of the king's affairs by a group of twenty-five barons. In Clause 61, the so-called security clause, John submits himself, as the monarch, to the judgement of these barons. This constituted a massive and radical challenge to the sovereign authority of the monarch, and it is therefore no surprise that when the document was reissued in 1225, that clause was absent.

The third principle of note is the extension of the liberties and rights contained within the charter to those who did not occupy the top strata of English society. Provisions made for "free men" occur in six of the charter's clauses (Clauses 15, 20, 27, 30, 34, 39), and Clause 60 concludes with an exhortation that the liberties in Magna Carta be extended to all by those in positions of authority. Although it wasn't until the fourteenth century that "all free men" would be extended to include those in positions of serfdom, and although the rights proclaimed in the 1215 version of Magna Carta were only ever granted as the concessions of a king, rather than being inherent or inalienable rights themselves, this extension of rights language remains deeply significant.

How did we get to this? How did we get to language of due process, of limitations to sovereignty, of rights language or talk of "all free men"? Most acutely, how did we get there in the thirteenth century, half a millennium before the so-called Enlightenment, in the midst of what we moderns like to think of as a period of brutality and barbarism?

4

The key is in the very first clause of the Charter, the promise of King John that "the English Church shall be free, and shall have its rights undiminished, and its liberties unimpaired." To our modern ears, trained to hear nothing but the sins of politicized religion, this sounds like a straightforward power-grab; the Church getting in there with its claims before anyone else could. And it was. But it was not only that. Or rather, that freedom of the Church, to which we shall return, is not only about the Church itself.

This is the point where we get to the first backstory concerning Magna Carta. The Church was central to the story of the Great Charter, though we should certainly not canonize its role. Pope Innocent III, whose time on the throne of Peter almost exactly coincided with John's on the English throne, had had a massive falling-out with the king early on, a falling-out so severe that the pope had placed an interdict on the whole country, prohibiting clergy from conducting religious services—something of a nuclear option in the ongoing battles between pope and crown in the middle ages.

This had eventually been settled and Innocent subsequently proved very helpful to John. In the wake of his first major run-in with barons in 1212, Innocent had helpfully declared England and Ireland to be papal fiefdoms. John thereby subjected himself and his lands not only to papal authority but also to papal protection—extremely powerful at this moment of history when the papacy was enjoying its greatest power. A few years later, in early 1215, the king made the (presumably empty) promise to take up the cross in crusade as a means of earning papal favor. It worked, and the maneuver won him Innocent's condemnation of the baronial rebellion. Safe in the knowledge that Pope Innocent III would find in his favor, King John then suggested that his dispute be arbitrated by a group of eight independent adjudicators, sitting under the direction of the pope. After Magna Carta was sealed, a mere two months after indeed, the king appealed to the pope, who found the Charter to comprise of promises made under duress, and then annulled it. All in all, the papacy, then somewhere close to its supreme powers, does not emerge as a shining defender of civil liberties.

But Innocent does not comprise the whole ecclesiastical story. John and Innocent had originally fallen out over who was to become archbishop of Canterbury in 1205. The pope wanted the Parisian theologian and biblical scholar Stephen Langton. John did not and refused, hence the interdict (and also John's excommunication). That was finally resolved when John backed down and Langton arrived in 1212.

Because of the way he eventually got to Canterbury, Langton was no natural ally of John. He saw himself as, and modelled himself on, the greatest priestly troublemaker of the age, St. Thomas Becket. Langton adopted an antagonistic stance toward the king (although not as antagonistic as a number of other English bishops and theologians who were far more vocal than the archbishop in promoting the rebel cause). Langton was no politician and had limited success against John in his various subsequent financial and political machinations.

But he did play a significant role in the negotiations between barons and kings, and while not quite a barons' man, was not as friendly to the king as Pope Innocent could be.

Langton served as something of a go-between for the two parties, helping ensure the barons got a fair hearing from the king (a role that is possibly reflected in the fact that he is named, in Clause 55, as a key arbiter in future disputes). After the Charter was annulled by the pope, Innocent demanded the excommunication of those barons who had made the demands of the king. Langton refused and was sent back into exile by John. After John died in 1216, Stephen returned and became particularly influential in securing the 1225 reissue, which he issued with a sentence of excommunication against any king, officer, or baron who broke the Charter's laws.

From the outset it was bishops who played a vital role in distributing copies of the Charter in their dioceses. Later still, it was senior bishops and archbishops who were instrumental in securing Magna Carta's numerous reissues during the reign of King Henry III. In other words, behind accidents and agendas of baronial revolt, there is a significant story of what role Christianity played through the Church. It's a checkered story, but it does at least put Christianity back on Magna Carta's map.

5

Even this is an incomplete story, however, because behind this backstory is another one, where we get much closer to the real principles involved that have made Magna Carta famous around the world today.

Christianity's role was not restricted simply to ecclesiastical actors and institutions and negotiations but was probably greatest in the realm of ideas, in *theology*. This is all too often missed. At the beginning of the twentieth century it was widely assumed that Langton was the principal author of Magna Carta. One can easily see why. We have good reason to believe that the first clause, guaranteeing the English Church her traditional rights and liberties, has Langton's fingerprints on it. Similarly, as a scholar in Paris, Langton had used the book of Deuteronomy to expound his belief in the need for a *written form of law* that would set out the rightful activity of kings and constrain their habitual excesses. *Only lawful action could be right action,* a view that was clearly very important in the formation of Magna Carta.

That view of Langton's authorship has now fallen firmly out of favor. The truth is we simply don't know who wrote what in the document. That notwithstanding, the Christian influence on the Charter goes beyond penmanship to the subtler world of ideas. Magna Carta was written after, and drew on, a century of ongoing development of (a theologically reflective and coherent) canon law. This was a great renewal and systematization of theological and legal thought (best embodied by a book by Gratian entitled *Decretum*, otherwise known as the *Concordance of Discordant Canons*). It provided intellectual foundations for key aspects of Magna Carta, as we can see by looking again at the three key principles we highlighted earlier.

The first is the question of due process within a legal framework, a major theological concern for Stephen Langton himself. The question of what was lawful in the public realm remained a topic of much debate among even the most conservative theologians. How far should Christians be "subject to the governing authorities"? Clearly a temporal ruler could not compel a Christian to renounce allegiance to Christ. How far then, for example, should Christians obey a ruler who commanded that which ran contrary to the will of God in other areas of the political life?

A number of examples were popular. How exactly, theologians asked, should a Christian respond to someone unjustly condemned to die by the king? How should a Christian respond to an unjust declaration of war by the king (a question that never seems to lose its relevance)? Langton provided the same response for both situations. The king should be obeyed, even by a Christian charged with the execution of an innocent party, but *only as long as the king's sentence has been passed by a legitimate court.* Others drew a similar answer but drew more directly still on Scripture. Pierre de Chanter, for example, Stephen Langton's mentor, argued from the book of Samuel—in which the prophet inscribes the law of the land in a book, to mark the coronation of King Saul—that the king was constrained by adherence to that law. Either way, the conclusion was the same and had great implications for Magna Carta: the king must be under law.

The second principle was to do with the legitimacy of action taken against king. The presence of the security clause in the 1215 issue of

Magna Carta, which put the king's affairs under baronial scrutiny, was highly unusual. In the history of Western law, it is one of the earliest—if not the very first—examples of a legal framework that held the monarchy to account for the fulfilment of its promises. This idea drew on a book written by the cleric John of Salisbury fifty years earlier, entitled *Policraticus*, which, in its many hundreds of pages, contains a number of highly influential reflections on what can and should be done about tyrannical rulers.

John offered an extended discussion on what is the true nature of a prince by drawing on repeated stories of bad kings in the Old Testament, who fell under God's judgement. He even went as far as to advocate punishing tyrants. "It is not only permitted, but it is also equitable and just to slay tyrants," he writes at one point. Because of John of Salisbury, and a few others like him, the intellectual and theological context of the early thirteenth century would have been fertile ground for the legitimation of direct action against a king who had failed to uphold due process and the laws of the land. It was because of these ideas that Clause 61 of Magna Carta could draw a direct link between the king's duty to follow the law of Magna Carta and the duty of the king's subjects to pay fealty to their monarch. The obedience of the people depended on the obedience of the king.

The third principle is in the famous extension of rights to "all free men." Clause 60 reads:

> All these customs and liberties that we have granted shall be observed in our kingdom in so far as concerns our own relations with our subjects. Let all men of our kingdom, whether clergy or laymen, observe them similarly in their relations with their own men.

This extension of rights is not a simple afterthought at the end of the Charter. It is something that frames the whole of Magna Carta, appearing right at the beginning in the first clause—"to all free men of our kingdom we have also granted, for us and our heirs for ever, all the liberties written out below"—and indeed throughout the intervening clauses.

This, it is worth repeating, is no expression of inalienable, fundamental or inherent human rights. "All free men" does not equal all men, let alone all people. The majority of peasants under the English feudal system were serfs, men and women who were bound—either through promise or inheritance—to a particular plot of land, owned by a particular lord. Although not technically slaves, neither were they free. Nevertheless, this extension of rights language to all minor landowners and tenants was highly unusual in the early thirteenth century and unparalleled in contemporary charters and statutes across Europe.

This language and understanding of rights had undergone significant development in the latter half of the twelfth century, particularly within the Church. Gratian's *Decretum* treated all persons as equal before the natural law of God. The natural law, as articulated by Gratian, refused to differentiate between persons based on their status, for the golden rule commands that everyone do to others as they would have done to themselves. If all persons stood equally before natural law, however, and if natural law formed the basis of human law, then the unavoidable implication was that all persons should also stand equal before human law.

This egalitarian line of thinking would go on to mark a subtle shift in the way medieval Europe thought about whom the law was intended to serve. Rather than serve the king or the state in the preservation of the "natural" social order, the law came to be seen as an instrument of justice intended to serve the whole populace. Thus Pope Innocent III—of all people—writing in 1204, would declare:

> It may be said that kings are to be treated differently from others. We, however, know that it is written in the divine law, "You shall judge the great as well as the little and there shall be no difference of persons."

That was rhetoric, perhaps, but it was nonetheless powerful rhetoric; and when powerful rhetoric escapes like this, especially when it is firmly grounded in a holy text, it often takes on a life of its own.

We need to be clear about what claims are being made here. Just as Christianity's role in the actual creation of Magna Carta via Church and churchmen is unclear and checkered, so its role in the formation of the Great Charter through ideas and theology is mixed and therefore contentious. We should not imagine we can see indisputable commitment to the inalienable dignity of all human beings enshrined in law in Magna Carta, or that we can trace an easy line of descent to those modern documents like the Universal Declaration of Human Rights that do articulate such a commitment.

That recognized, Christianity's role in the development of Magna Carta, particularly in cultivating the intellectual hinterland on which it drew, is significant and very important. We ignore it at the peril of amnesia and historical dishonesty. In recognition of the fact that he who controls the past controls the present and he who controls the present controls the future, we should not airbrush the role of Christianity out of the history of this most seminal of legal documents, for fear that it will make it easier to airbrush Christianity out of our present and future.

6

Can we draw any contemporary lessons from this, or is it all merely a matter of historical interest? Let me end with one suggestion.

Magna Carta and the legal culture in which it grew were profoundly shaped by the Church; not just by Christian beliefs but by an institution that was shaped (in theory) by those beliefs and protected itself fiercely from outward interference with them and it.

Once again, we should not be under any illusion here. Innocent III was no saint. Stephen Langton was no saint. St. Thomas Beckett was no saint (despite what people thought at the time—indeed, Beckett did more for the Church by dying than he ever did when alive, and the only people to dislike and distrust him more than Henry II were his own bishops).

But even if they were self-interested (and I don't suggest they were *solely* self-interested), the fact remains that it was the existence of the Church as an independent, self-governing body that forced political rulers to recognize a space that was not under their immediate jurisdiction. The fact that this institution was committed (in theory) to universal and equal dignity for all, and that it also proclaimed a message that the king was under God's law and judgement, added to this strength.

Freedom was gained in the West by people *taking* liberties, and in the first instance that meant having an institution that was big and rich and tough and self-assured enough to stand in the way of what was, effectively, the absolute power and wealth of monarch and emperor. It was this that, in the long run, led to the carving out of what we would call today civil society, that arena where groups and organizations and institutions operate, between the individual and the state, without requiring the permission of the latter to exist.

Now, only the most apocalyptic think we have lost that today. However, one does not have to be apocalyptic to recognize that our political health is not what it might be. "We don't do institutions"—to coin a phrase. The organizational infrastructure that so dominated British social life until the mid-twentieth century—churches, chapels, political parties, trade unions, mutuals, cooperatives, associations, and the like—is much weaker today. If you think filling a church is difficult, you want to try filling a local branch meeting for a political party.

The result is that we have declined into a rhetorical pattern in which there are two main actors on our social stage—the state and the individual, with all relations between and within those groups being mediated through market interactions or the law.

The problems with the first of these are well documented, as I discuss in a later chapter on Thomas Piketty's blockbuster *Capital in the Twenty-First Century*. The market might be a realm of unparalleled efficiency, but it is also one of seemingly inevitable inequality, where whoever has will be given more, and whoever does not have, even what they have will be taken from them.

The problem with the latter is, perhaps, less self-evident. Law after all is a good thing. That is what Magna Carta tells us. But perhaps it's not necessarily a good thing. Perhaps it's only a good thing when used to do the things that law should be used to do.

A High Court judge is not the first place you would naturally look for a criticism of the law, but Lord Sumption's 2013 lecture on the limits of the law puts this very well.

> We live in an age of unbounded confidence in the value and efficacy of law as an engine of social and moral improvement. The spread of parliamentary democracy across most of the world has invariably been followed by rising public expectations of the state, of which the courts are a part.

The result of this here may be seen in the vast increase in criminal and regulatory offences on the UK statute book—an estimated 3,000 in the Tony Blair decade alone. But this is not necessarily a good thing. More law does not mean a better society, particularly if that law actually encroaches on things that are properly speaking political—areas of genuine and reasonable difference.

Sumption gives the example of the European Convention for the Protection of Human Rights and Fundamental Freedoms to illustrate this. This is a "living instrument." In other words, it "allows it to make new law in respects which are not foreshadowed by the language of the Convention and which Parliament would not necessarily have anticipated when it passed the Act":

> The effect of this kind of judicial lawmaking is in constitutional terms rather remarkable. It is to take many contentious issues which would previously have been regarded as questions for political debate, administrative discretion or social convention and transform them into questions of law to be resolved by an international judicial tribunal.

In other words, if we want to put this in more concrete terms and allude to a contentious issues such as the question of prisoner voting, this is not simply a question of whether prisoners should be entitled to vote but also about *who should decide* whether they should: Parliament or those "judges in Strasbourg."

Too much law may be problematic in the way that too little law is. More precisely, when matters that are deeply and properly contentious—like prisoner voting—are subject not to parliamentary debate but to legal adjudication, especially when that legal adjudication feels rather distant from the population in question, it badly undermines people's faith in democracy—of which they haven't got much in the first place.

The reasons why we have inclined toward this attitude to the law are complicated but they have much to do with the decline of religion and other cultural powers. In Sumption's words:

> other restraints on the autonomy and self-interest of men, such as religion and social convention, have lost much of their former force, at any rate in the West. The role of social and religious sentiment, which was once so critical in the life of our societies, has been largely taken over by law.

This is an interesting and important corrective to the Magna Carta view of history. Law, as Magna Carta illustrates, is important. Law is essential. Law is necessary. But law is not sufficient. It is not enough.

Magna Carta was made possible by the fact of the Church, and even if the Church was an imperfect and hypocritical institution, it still preached the social and cultural norms without which even the best laws in the world would be powerless. In the absence of those deep cultural norms, those religious and social conventions, which were historically embedded in institutions, there is a temptation to turn to the law to settle all disputes. And if that law is somehow seen as extra-political—as it clearly is today when you are dealing with "living instruments" like the European Convention for the Protection of Human Rights and Fundamental Freedoms—then not only is society weakened but so, ultimately, is democracy.

4

Christianity and Democracy: Friend and Foe

————•◦•————

1

The stories told about the relationship between Christianity and democracy usually fall into one of two well-worn types.

The first is the claim that all our democratic freedoms are owed to Christianity, in general, and Protestant Christianity specifically. This argument is both sociological and historical. It invites us to look at those nations with the longest continuous traditions of democratic freedom, then at those with little or no comparable tradition, then at those that have made the transition between the two, and it then invites us to trace the common and unifying themes.

This had been done a number of times, drawing on quantitative data where available, and the studies repeatedly show that those countries with a Protestant inheritance, either indigenously or by post-colonial inheritance, show the longest history and greatest degree of democratic freedom. Studies also show that the so-called Third Wave of democratization that began in 1974, with the fall of Estado Novo's regime in Portugal, was strongly correlated to Catholicism. In contrast, those countries with no Christian heritage and, in particular, those countries with a strong Islamic culture and polity, have come very late to the party, if they have come at all.

This, of course, is not a new argument, even if the empirical contribution is a recent one. Indeed, in some respects it is nearly two hundred years old. Alexis de Tocqueville's *Democracy in America*, published between 1835 and 1840, made great play of the fact that religion was the foundation for democracy in America, rather than its irreconcilable antagonist, as it had been in his native France.

The second argument is that all our democratic freedoms are owed to our *emancipation* from Christianity. This has taken the status of some kind of secular creation myth, which recounts how a terrible theocratic monster once terrorized land and people until a few brave, liberal-minded, and determinedly secular philosophers slew it with new-forged weapons of reason and science.

It is colorful polemic, but like all good polemic it has more than a grain of truth in it. One of the major scholarly achievements in European history over recent years is Jonathan Israel's massive and outstanding three-part history of the Enlightenment, in which he traces the impact of philosophical ideas and, in particular, radical philosophical ideas on the formation of the European mind between the end of the Thirty Years War in 1648 and the French Revolution in 1789. In this story, the Jewish philosopher Baruch Spinoza plays a seminal role, although on account of his radical, monistic philosophy rather than his Jewishness. Israel's argument is that all that characterizes the modern world, including democratic freedom, secularism, human rights, and toleration, comes from the Radical Enlightenment generally and Spinoza specifically, most of it fought for in opposition to the Christian orthodoxy of the time.

Critics of Israel's thesis—and they are increasing in number—have pointed out that it does sound like a bit of a creation narrative itself. Thus a review of the first two books of the trilogy in *The Nation* began:

> Humanity lived in darkness—until He came. In the beginning only a few rallied to his cause. It was too enigmatic to arouse much popular support, and political opposition forced its champions underground. But a coterie of apostles resolved to spread a simplified version of his good news against stiff-necked enemies who often made martyrs of them. Then something remarkable happened. Thanks to a collection of gospels about his morality, the zealous devotion of followers and, of course, the obvious truth of his good news, his call for emancipation spread far beyond his native land and eventually set the world on fire.

"He," of course, is Baruch Spinoza.

Israel's argument is effectively that the indisputable link between Protestant cultures and the growth of democratic freedom is not due to Protestantism. It wasn't Christianity that bred democracy. Rather, it was only in Protestant cultures that secularism was able to get a foothold, and it is to secularism and not Protestantism that we owe our commitment to democracy.

These twin claims, or narratives, are substantial and do not lend themselves to straightforward adjudication. It is fair to say, however, that neither tale is gospel, so to speak. Both arguments have something to them and neither has the monopoly on truth. On balance my view is closer to the first story than the second—that Christianity and democracy are strongly and causally linked. But that narrative alone, even if it is the truth, is certainly not the whole truth. Christianity has been neither an unqualified friend nor an unqualified foe to democracy.

Rather, it has been a friend *and* a foe, a complex relationship that I want to unpack by engaging on a brief tour of their relationship in English and British history. One can hardly hope to do this comprehensively in a single chapter, so I will instead make three stops— looking first at the Christian basis of *political authority* as articulated in early English history; second, at the Christian basis for *political liberty* as articulated in the Reformation and post-Reformation periods; and third at the Christian basis for *democratic liberty*, as articulated in the nineteenth century—before concluding with a few remarks on the role of Christianity in British democracy today.

2

We begin with the very idea of what political power is for. What, in other words, makes a king, emperor, or any ruler, legitimate?

The Bible has—or can be quoted to justify—a very high view of political power. Old Testament kings were anointed, thereby sanctifying them with the very authority of God. The New Testament is, superficially at least, highly deferential to the powers that be, Romans 13 being the proof-text of choice: "Whosoever therefore resisteth the power, resisteth the ordinance of God" (KJV).

Such views underpinned the view of emperor that persisted in the Eastern Roman empire, in which "the imperial rank" was exempted from legislation because the emperor was himself "a living law." The collapse of the Roman empire took history in a different direction in the West, however. There, royal power was still validated on Christian grounds and coronation services marked with ritual anointing from at least the eighth century. However, the closeness of the Eastern link between empire and Church was never quite replicated in the West, with churchmen claiming and sometimes exercising the right to stand apart from and to judge monarchs. This meant that the question about when was a king not a king lay with churchmen, who were sometimes willing to deploy it critically. In other words, the Christian basis for political authority in Western Europe from the mid-first millennium onwards was a twofold one: it legitimized kingship and, in the process, it limited it.

The first of these—Christianity's legitimization of kingship—is very easy to demonstrate from the sources. King Wihtred of Kent issued a law code in AD 695 that had twenty-eight decrees in it. The first one proclaimed, "The Church [is to be] free from taxation. And the king is to be prayed for, and they are to honor him of their own free-will without compulsion." Putting aside the irony of *legislating* for prayer "without compulsion," this little piece of legislature offers a gloriously clear picture of the origins of a mutually beneficial arrangement between state and Church, throne and altar, that dominated European politics for the next 1,100 years.

The early English repeatedly drew on the Old Testament, with its extensive history of kings and kingship, to demonstrate the divine origins of royal power. The fact that the Old Testament is, in fact, profoundly ambivalent about kingship was usually glossed over. In legitimizing the king's rule, however, the Church also began the process of limiting it. Ironically, this process was linked very closely to the fact of legitimization. If Christianity legitimized political authority, the answer to the question of what made a king legitimate was therefore, at root, a Christian one. Kings were kings not by force of arms or even inheritance, but by the grace of God. "[It was] not your own merit but the abundant goodness of God [that] appointed king and rule over many," St. Boniface told King Aethelbert of Mercia.

If kings were only kings on account of the "goodness of God," it meant that they had to pay attention to his terms and conditions. In the early middle ages the accountability of the king before God meant that kings were regularly reminded of their duties by the clergy who preached, wrote to them, or drafted their legislation. "Ponder . . . within yourself how diligently to establish God's law over the people of God," Cathwulf urged the greatest of all early European rulers, Charlemagne.

This placed upon kings certain specified duties. These varied but they included the protection of God's Holy Church, undoubtedly the king's foremost duty, at least in the eyes of God's Holy Churchmen, and defending and advancing the Christian faith—a responsibility that would lead down some ethically murky paths over the years. These are precisely the kind of things—self-interest and conversion by compulsion—that the popular mind associates with medieval kingship. But to stop there would be unfair and misleading. The legitimizing duties of kingship also included the duty to judge justly. The abbot Aelfric wrote in his *Treatise on the Old and New Testament,* "he who is God's servant should judge rightly with fairness without any payment." It demanded that the ruler govern with mercy. Alfred remarked in the introduction to his law code that

> when it came about that many people had received the faith of Christ, many synods were established throughout the earth, and likewise throughout the English people ... [and] they established, for that mercy which Christ taught, that secular lords might with their permission receive without sin compensation in money for almost every misdeed at the first offence.

It meant valuing life, reflecting a theological attitude that saw life as a gift that should not be disposed of too easily, either by death or by surrendering people into slavery, a genuine problem in the age of Viking raids. It meant there was a serious responsibility to secure peace, a hugely demanding challenge in cultures formed by a warrior ethic. It laid upon rulers the responsibility to protect the weak, especially the Old Testament triad of the poor, widows, and orphans. It required the imposition of law to which all, in theory, had unmediated access. Thus toward the end of the Anglo-Saxon period, King Ethelred's law code began, "it is the decree of our Lord and his councillors that just practices be established and all illegal practices abolished, and that every man is to be permitted the benefit of law."

Last but certainly not least in the mind of those Anglo-Saxon clerics to which we still have access, it required rulers to live a life of personal virtue. The same letter in which missionary bishops praised King Aethelbald for his charity concentrated, in some detail, on the king's sexual misdemeanors. The bishops would accept that the king had "never taken in matrimony a lawful wife," but only if he had also chosen to "maintain . . . chaste abstinence for God's sake." Aethelbald, however, had not. Instead he preferred a life of "lasciviousness and adultery . . . committed in the monasteries with holy nuns and virgins consecrated to God." The bishops were not pleased.

All this was, of course, theoretical. The practical reality was different, although perhaps not as different as the popular image of this period as a time of heroic barbarism would have it. However much such political strictures were honored in the breach rather than the observance, the theory remained important. Only if a king did this could he rightfully claim the mantle of king. Only then could his power be considered to be authority.

Put together, the responsibilities that Christianity placed upon the king—justice, peace, care for the weak, personal morality—gesture in the direction of a monarch who, while in no way contracted with his people, was placed in a political order that intimated that the legitimacy of his position was somehow dependent on the discharge of those duties. It was kingship under God, orientated, however hopefully, to the common good of the people.

It obviously took many centuries for the implications of this to be worked out in full. But once again, even here the reality was recognized by some of the more perceptive Anglo-Saxons themselves. In his *Treatise on the Old and New Testament*, Aelfric outlined the classic threefold division of medieval society—between laborers, clerics, and soldiers—and made the point that the health of the king and his kingdom depended on the health of each of these roles: "On these three supports the throne stands, and if one is broken down, it falls at once, certainly to the detriment of the other supports." It was a common theme. Around the same time Wulfstan, archbishop of York, remarked in a homily that "on these three pillars every throne shall stand upright in a Christian nation." If any of them weakens, he warned, "the throne will soon totter; and if any of them should break then the throne will fall and that will damage the people."

The apparent dependence of a kingdom's health on the extent to which its king served the good of the people would point, in the fullness of time, toward the need for the people themselves to agree to a particular monarch. Such an idea was hardly in the mind of those Anglo-Saxon ecclesiastics who wrote about the king being judged by God for his sins, but very occasionally they hinted at it. In a homily for Palm Sunday, delivered in the last years of the tenth century, Aelfric remarked that

> No man can make himself king, but the people has the choice to choose a king whom they please; but after he is consecrated as king, he then has dominion over the people, and they cannot shake his yoke from their necks.

This was an extraordinary idea for the time, not so very far from the ideas of Thomas Hobbes or John Locke over six centuries later. It is not democracy in any recognizable format but it is not hard to see how democratic accountability could emerge from it.

3

Given all this it is ironic to realize that such a strong commitment to justice for the common good could also actually impede rather than encourage a commitment to democracy. Put simply, if there was a right way and wrong way to govern, why risk allowing the people to choose the wrong way? If you were to bet on a political sentiment that was most likely to be found in an English bishop's mouth, right up until the mid-nineteenth century, this would surely be the favorite.

That recognized, democracy did evolve in Britain and the fact that it did so owes much to one of the least democratically minded Christian thinkers in the English tradition, William Tyndale. It is here we come to the basis for Christian political *liberty*. Tyndale was one of the most brilliant linguists and wordsmiths of the Reformation, but he was also about as far from a democrat as it is possible to be. His only substantial work of political theology, *The Obedience of a Christian Man*, embraced, almost without reservation, the extreme political authoritarianism that marked the early years of the Reformation.

Following Luther, Tyndale reasoned that the picture of a divinely ordained social order, with which he began that book, meant not only that subjects have a duty to obey their political masters but also that they must not even actively resist tyranny. "Neither may the inferior person avenge himself upon the superior, or violently resist him, for whatsoever wrong it be," he stated, before going on to explain that in doing so he "takes upon him that which belongs to God only." The duties of the king fitted into this context. Christian kings ought to "give themselves altogether to the wealth [welfare] of their realms after the ensample of Christ." They should "remember . . . that the people are God's, and not theirs," and that "the king is but a servant, to execute the law of God, and not to rule after his own imagination." Tyndale could even, on occasion, slip into the kind of rhetoric of radical equality that was in danger of confirming the accusations made against him and his fellow reformers. "The most despised person in his realm is the king's brother, and fellow-member with him, and equal with him in the kingdom of God and of Christ." Such radical equality notwithstanding, however, Tyndale's practical teaching was one of undiluted authoritarianism and obedience.

Tyndale the political theorist was matched—and badly undermined—by Tyndale the evangelical, however. As an evangelical, which is how the early Reformers identified themselves, Tyndale's overwhelming concern was to make the Scriptures accessible to everyone in their own language, no matter how poor or socially browbeaten they were. Living and working as a tutor in Gloucestershire in the early 1520s, he is said to have remarked to a learned clergyman over dinner, "If God spare my life ere many years I will cause a boy that drives the plough shall know more of the Scripture than you do." Not only did this put before all manner of classes the very founding documents of society and encourage them to read and discuss them, but it simultaneously removed the safe, guiding hand of the learned and ordained. So important was it to clear a path for the unmediated relationship between God and the individual believer, that it was worth risking political disorder in order to enable that religious freedom.

Tyndale never lived to translate the whole Bible, though his masterly rendition of the New Testament was the rock on which the King James Version's translators built. Nor did he live to see Thomas Cromwell pass an injunction instructing parish priests to provide a Bible in their churches, and telling them to "admonish every man to read the same as the very word of God." The interesting thing about this epochal edict, however, was how quickly the authorities tried to row back from it. The idea of widespread biblical reading and engagement soon soured. It was simply too dangerous. Almost as soon as parishes were ordered to keep a Bible for the people to read, Henry VIII started passing restrictions on Bible reading. Too many people—in particular too many of the wrong sort of people—were too enthusiastic, reading, digesting, and, worse, disagreeing about biblical teaching.

A 1541 proclamation ordering the Great Bible to be placed in churches also commanded that "lay subjects" should not "presume to take upon them any common disputation, argument, or exposition of the mysteries therein contained." It was a case of shutting the stable door far too late. Two years later the Act for the Advancement of True Religion forbade subjects "of the lower sort" from reading the Bible, declaring:

> no women [although some noblewomen were exempted] nor artificers, prentices, journeymen, serving men of the degrees of yeoman or under, husbandmen, nor laborers shall read the Bible or New Testament to himself or any other, privately or openly.

The political implications of this should be clear. What Reformation Protestantism insisted on was a form of spiritual democracy in which everyone, no matter how lowly, was entitled to access the founding documents of their faith and decide for themselves how they should live and worship. Conscience reigned supreme.

The authorities saw in this potentially chaotic implications for national order, and they were right. Those moments before the late seventeenth century when the system of church courts and of censorship finally broke down saw publications and groups emerge into the light when most people preferred they stayed in the dark. During the civil war and Interregnum of the 1640s and '50s, for the first time in English history anyone who wanted to get into print—and who could persuade a printer that there was profit in the publication—could. And it was here that spiritual democracy came home to roost.

Reacting against Oliver Cromwell's negotiations with Charles I after the first civil war, in which a conservative and Presbyterian settlement for the nation was discussed, the Levellers published *The Case of the Army Truly Stated*, in which they wrote:

> God hath given no man a talent to be wrapped up in a napkin and not improved, but the meanest vassal (in the eye of the world) is equally obliged, and accountable to God, with the greatest prince or commander under the sun in and for the use of that talent be trusted unto him.

In a similar document, *Agreement of the People*, the authors advocated a redrawing of constituencies to better suit the population, biannual elections, a ban on conscription, universal obedience to the law, and religious toleration and freedom of religious conscience. These ideas were subsequently debated at Putney Church in October and November 1647, in which some participants, most famously Colonel Thomas Rainsborough, articulated some impeccably democratic sentiments.

> For really I think that the poorest he that is in England hath a life to live, as the greatest he; and therefore truly, sir, I think it's clear, that every man that is to live under a government ought first by his own consent to put himself under that government; and I do think that the poorest man in England is not at all bound in a strict sense to that government that he hath not had a voice to put himself under.

Rainsborough's argument was extreme even for such a radical time but it has been justly remembered and widely quoted. Less widely acknowledged is the fact that these sentiments would have been impossible without the life and work of one of the earliest English Reformers, who would himself have been horrified at them.

4

Such sentiments, which paralleled and drew on similar debates about church government, were quickly abandoned with the restoration of the monarchy in 1660. But they were not entirely forgotten and were drawn on in the battle for democracy in the nineteenth century. They stand as an example of how the political liberty accidentally implicit within Reformation Christianity prepared the ground for democratic liberty two or so centuries later.

Once again, this was a battle of two Christian halves. In the same way as Anglo-Saxon England saw Christianity legitimize and limit political authority, and Reformation England saw it preach a message of political obedience and of political freedom, so when the battle for the Reform Bill was on in the early nineteenth century, Christians were deeply split, mainly along social—which were also at the time denominational—lines.

On one side were the bishops. They were at the forefront of the anti-reform movement. Although they said comparatively little about the Great Reform Act of 1832 at the time (only one spoke during the second reading in 1831), twenty-one voted against the bill and only two supported it. The crowds were furious, demanding disestablishment and attacking bishops' palaces. At the second reading the following year, the bishops were more vocal but also more divided, twelve voting for the bill and fifteen against it.

On the other side were Christian political radicals. Early nineteenth-century Christian radicals argued powerfully (and biblically), repeatedly drawing on the idea of a spiritual democracy to defend a political one. Some radicals used this kind of logic to argue for an extended franchise. John Wade's *Black Book* of 1820 described Christ as "the great radical reformer of Israel—waging fearless war with the bloated hypocrites, who, under the mask of religion and holiness, devoured in idleness the rewards of virtuous industry." Another radical, John Cartwright, called Jesus "the Great Reformer" and argued that just as Jesus had laid the foundations for Christianity among the poor, so should parliamentary reform be extended to include such poor. If, Cartwright argued, God considered even the humblest man competent to judge for himself the means of eternal salvation, and good laws were simply the means of temporal salvation, it followed that the English constitution should involve the people in legislation. Here was Tyndale's ambition for even the ploughboy to know Scripture and salvation for himself returning with political vengeance.

Christian history was put to similar effect. In his 1820 publication *Why Are We Poor?*, the pseudonymous Roger Radical argued that the laboring classes were like the "primitive Christians . . . when all the potentates of the earth, all the rich, and the grandees were their enemies, and cruelly persecuted them to death, or to captivity, dungeons, and tortures of every description." Moreover, just as Christ and Christian history were used against the establishment, so were the Prayer Book and the Christian creeds. Various publications parodied catechisms, creeds, and prayers as a way of invoking the notion of true, democratically inclined, biblical religion as against that of established Church.

The most famous instance was that of William Hone, whose work ended up marking a significant moment in the freedom of the press. Hone grew up in a traditional, Bible-dominated household in the 1780s, although he moved away from his childhood orthodoxy in the wake of the Revolution in France. He worked as a bookseller, publisher, satirist, and journalist, although his business ventures were rarely successful. In 1817, his short-lived journal *The Reformists' Register* attacked establishment hypocrisies and ridiculed leading public figures by means of parodying the liturgy and the Athanasian Creed. He was tried for his efforts, on the grounds that bringing the Prayer Book and Christianity into contempt harmed public morals. However, he defended himself well, adopting a deliberately Christian stance during his trial, repeatedly referring to Christ as "Our Savior" and accusing his persecutors of neglecting the true precepts of Christianity. Despite standing before hostile judges he was acquitted.

Christian political reformers walked a dangerous line. On the one hand they were distrusted by secular radicals who thought they couldn't be truly reformist because they were Christian, and on the other hand they were distrusted by the Christian authorities who thought they couldn't be truly Christian because they were reformist. Moreover, by this point in national history, the political stage was crowded with ideas that hadn't been there in the post-Reformation period, let alone the Anglo-Saxon. Christian arguments were no longer decisive (even assuming they once were), and the Christian arguments for an extended franchise in Britain from the 1830s onwards took their place among many other, sometimes hostile, agendas. But the arguments were nonetheless powerful, and they contributed, through the nineteenth century and beyond, to the transformation of British political life and to that of nations that had been formed, or at least informed, by Protestantism.

5

This brings us to our current day and to a conclusion. We enthusiastically genuflect before the altar of democracy today in much the same way as we did before the altar of nationalism a century ago. And yet, in both circumstances, there is hollowness in our piety. Just as our great-grandparents, or many of them, could be perfectly devout about those things that left them feeling comfortable, so we deem democracy sacrosanct and spread that gospel worldwide, while we have poor turnouts for national elections, disgraceful ones for European and local ones; unbridled cynicism about our democratically elected politicians; and desperately low levels of party membership and activity. In the light of this, proposals such as the democratization of the House of Lords or state funding for political parties would be funny if they weren't actually serious.

There are many reasons for this democratic deficit and overwhelming sense of cynicism, and many more solutions, all of which are beyond the scope of this chapter. However else we might respond, though, perhaps a lesson that may be drawn from Christianity's checkered engagement with democratic freedom in Britain over the years, is to temper our democratic genuflection. The voting booth is not some kind of political wardrobe that permits us into a social Narnia. The people on the other side of the election process are as fallible— sometimes conspicuously more so—as those who put them there. Incorporating the public's view as to what comprises the public good is essential, and we should make friends of those political systems that enable it. But it is a very long way from being the answer to all our woes, and we should beware of any sense that such political systems are salvific in this way. If Christianity has been a friend and a foe to democracy, it is perhaps because democracy has the potential to be friend and foe to true human flourishing.

5

Saving Humanism from the Humanists

―――•·•·•―――

1

It is a peculiarity of modern English, which would have puzzled our grandparents, that the word "humanist" has come to mean "non-" or even "anti-religious."

In 1928, T. S. Eliot wrote an essay on the humanism of the American literary critic Irving Babbitt. The essay irked Babbitt, who responded by claiming that Eliot had "misstated" his views. Eliot replied the following year saying that his essay "was not intended to be an attack [on humanism]" but rather "to point out the weak points in its defences, before some genuine enemy took advantage of them . . . There is no opposition between the religious and the pure humanistic attitude," Eliot claimed. "They are necessary to each other."

This was hardly an anomalous position. The interwar years had seen publications like the *Humanism and the Bible* series in Protestant circles. More influential, although not in the Anglophone world, was the work of the French neo-Thomist philosopher Jacques Maritain, whose book *True* (later *Integral) Humanism*, published in 1938, was profoundly important to the evolving theology of the post-war Catholic world. Christianity and humanism could be awkward bedfellows but there was little sign that divorce was imminent.

That divorce occurred was due in some measure to Christians rather than atheists. In 1945 the Church of England report *Towards the Conversion of England* took several sideswipes at "humanism," choosing to understand it in its narrower form. "Humanism is the word now commonly used to describe that view of life which sees in man the source of all meaning and value, instead of God," the report wrote with only partial truth. Such an interpretation helped effect a detachment and then separation, which was further ensured by the educationalist Harold Blackham, who helped steer the ethical movement away from its religious forms and toward outright godlessness. What had once been a capacious and generous ideology consonant with—arguably dependent on—Christian ideas, became narrower, more intolerant, and more anti-religious.

2

Humanism's prehistory lies in the classical world, in the Latin term *humanitas*, meaning human nature, in the sense of a civilized—as opposed to barbarian—human nature. Although sometimes used to mean philanthropy, it was more often deployed to indicate the kind of speech and education that befitted a cultivated man.

It was this sense that was developed in the Renaissance, and although such learning could be in tension with late-medieval scholasticism or the Reformation's stress on *sola scriptura*, the fact was that, in Diarmaid MacCulloch's words, "the vast majority of humanists were patently sincere Christians who wished to apply their enthusiasm to the exploration and proclamation of their faith."

The word "humanist" first appears in English in the later sixteenth century and subsequently oscillated between this idea of the individual as grammarian or rhetorician and the related but broader one of the individual as student of human affairs. When the first publication to be titled *The Humanist* appeared in 1757, the editor, an Irish clergyman, wrote that "the title . . . implies neither more nor less, than that it interests itself in all the concerns of human nature." It lasted fifteen issues.

Humanism began to accrete a more complex and religiously antagonistic set of connotations in the nineteenth century. The disciples of the philosopher Georg Hegel, known as the Young or Left Hegelians, introduced a specific non-Christian element to the idea of humanism in the second quarter of the century. One of them, Ludwig Feuerbach, explicitly put humanity in place of God, as the only object truly worthy of reverence, and his contemporary, Arnold Ruge, adopted humanism—alongside other terms like "anthropotheism"— to describe this shift. Humanism was, in effect, the culmination of Christianity, the religion's primitive supernaturalism being like a skin that had to be shed as humanity progressed.

Simultaneously, the French thinkers Henri de Saint-Simon and Auguste Comte developed a full-blooded Religion of Humanity, more commonly known as Positivism, which sought to deify humanity—although in a way more explicit and more colorful than anything Ruge attempted. Their efforts provoked high-minded loyalty and much mockery.

A little later, the historians Georg Voigt and Jacob Burckhardt used the word, entirely properly, when describing the ideology of the Italian Renaissance, but did so in such a way as implied a complete break with the (so-called) middle ages. In this manner, in the words of the historian J. A. Symonds in 1877, the idea that "the essence of humanism consisted in a new and vital perception of the dignity of man as a rational being apart from theological considerations" was born.

Between them these various conceptions of humanism introduced a more self-consciously anti-Christian element to the idea, although it is worth noting that humanism was still far too religious a term to appeal to the nascent anti-Christian movement of nineteenth-century Britain, which preferred instead to talk of free thought, atheism, naturalism, rationalism, and secularism.

Comte's Positivism, in its early, French, incarnation, did have a small impact in Britain, morphing eventually into what would be called the Ethical Movement, which retained many of the religious overtones and ideas of its parent movement while jettisoning traditional theistic elements.

Even those self-proclaimed rationalists more naturally antagonistic to the religious origins and feel of the ethical movement spoke of humanism in religious terms. "Humanism!" exclaimed Charles Hooper, first secretary of the Rationalist Press Association in 1900, "What one word could be better adapted to mark the gospel which is a gospel at once of human knowledge, of human nature, and of human society?"

Such was the complex web of ideas and beliefs that comprised the "humanism" of which Eliot wrote in the 1920s, a capacious and inclusive family of ideas ranging from the Christian, through the quasi-Christian right all the way to the anti-Christian. In the words of S. H. Swinny, then president of the London Positivist Society and editor of the *Positivist Review*, "we certainly claim no proprietary right in the word Humanist [and] we welcome all to the Humanist name."

3

This capacious understanding narrowed in the second half of the twentieth century, as we have noted, and although some atheists have recognized the breadth of the term, others have asserted a fierce sense of anti-religious ownership. "Humanism [is] an alternative to religion," stated the father of modern atheistic humanism Harold Blackham with admirable bluntness in 1967.

Such humanism may be anti-religious, but precisely what it is pro- is less clear. Different answers abound. According to Blackham, it proceeds from "an assumption that man is on his own and this life is all and an assumption of responsibility for one's own life and for the life of mankind." In the words of the novelist Kurt Vonnegut, "being a humanist means trying to behave decently without expectation of rewards or punishment after you are dead." Others have associated it with "reason, decency, tolerance, empathy" (Jim Al-Khalili, president of the British Humanist Association), or with "the intense wonder and beauty of the universe" (Professor Brian Cox), or with the capacity of human agency and potential, or with free intellectual enquiry.

"The fullest definition to have a measure of international agreement," at least according to the British Humanist Association, is the 2002 Amsterdam Declaration of the International Humanist and Ethical Union (IHEU), which was developed on the fiftieth anniversary of the first World Humanist Congress and the original Amsterdam Declaration, and was "adopted unanimously" by the IHEU General Assembly, thereby becoming "the official defining statement of World Humanism." A long definition—over 500 words in fact—it contains seven clauses outlining the "fundamentals of modern Humanism," which state (in brief) that humanism (1) is ethical; (2) is rational; (3) supports democracy and human rights; (4) insists that personal liberty must be combined with social responsibility; (5) is a response to the widespread demand for an alternative to dogmatic religion; (6) values artistic creativity and imagination; and (7) is a lifestance aiming at the maximum possible fulfilment.

It will be immediately obvious that neither the religious nor the irreligious hold any monopoly here and that it seems impossible, even in the fullest declaration, to define humanism in an exclusive way. It is not far from this to the conclusion that we should be prepared to settle for a generous and inclusive humanism, shared by believer and non-believer alike, and that, as the atheist humanist Nicolas Walter remarks in his little book *Humanism: What's in the Word*, published by the Rationalist Press Association, "attempts to control books and words almost never succeed."

4

In one regard this is entirely correct and precisely what we need. However, even when one acknowledges that there are a variety of legitimate foundations for humanism, there is still the awkward question about which ideology best supports humanist ideals. Some, such as valuing artistic creativity and imagination, may not require any significant intellectual substructure, but others, such as the commitment to reliable rationality, the sense of ethical realism, and, perhaps most importantly, a commitment to the "human," do.

At the core of humanism is, self-evidently, the word, the concept, and a serious commitment to "the human." Humanists, both religious and atheist, talk about the "dignity" or "value" or "worth" or "sanctity" of human beings, or of human life or of the human "person." They often place this commitment at the heart of their ethical thinking (although in different ways), and many seek to establish and secure it legally through a range of specific, named human rights.

The British Humanist Association has as one of its values "recognising the dignity of individuals and treating them with fairness and respect." The so-called 1991 "Minimum Statement" of the International Humanist and Ethical Union explains how humanism stands for the building of a "more humane society" through an ethic "based on human and other natural values."* The 2002 IHEU Amsterdam Declaration affirms the "worth, dignity and autonomy of the individual."

---

* The Minimum Statement is a little opaque here. Competitiveness and belligerence are, after all, thoroughly "human" and "natural" traits that have been and are deeply valued by certain individuals and cultures, but it is doubtful they could play any significant role in building a humane society.

This commitment to human dignity or worth is not simply a theoretical issue, of concern only to moral philosophers. Indeed, it is central to one of the most famous documents of the twentieth century. The Preamble to the Universal Declaration of Human Rights begins by recognizing "the inherent dignity and the equal and inalienable rights of all members of the human family" as "the foundation of freedom, justice and peace in the world," and goes on to talk about the "faith" that the peoples of the United Nations have in "the dignity and worth of the human person and in the equal rights of men and women."

The Universal Declaration, however, also—famously—fails to *justify* this faith in human dignity, or rather does so only in negative, historically specific, or aspirational terms. Thus the Preamble declares how "disregard and contempt for human rights have resulted in barbarous acts which have outraged the conscience of mankind," and how "if man is not to be compelled to have recourse, as a last resort, to rebellion against tyranny and oppression . . . human rights should be protected by the rule of law." Similarly, it speaks of the "advent" of a world in which "human beings shall enjoy freedom of speech and belief and freedom from fear and want," which "has been proclaimed as the highest aspiration of the common people."

The Preamble's commitment to and justification for human dignity are intelligible but strangely unsatisfying. "Because we live in the shadow of evil . . . , because it is better for all of us if we respect human dignity . . . , because we aspire to freedom from fear and want . . . ": these are admirable but fall short of being philosophically—or ethically—compelling.

This has long been recognized. Jacques Maritain, the aforementioned Catholic humanist who was instrumental in the drafting of the Universal Declaration of Human Rights, subsequently remembered that at one of the meetings of a UNESCO National Commission where human rights were being discussed, "someone expressed astonishment that certain champions of violently opposed ideologies had agreed on a list of those rights. 'Yes,' they said, 'we agree about the rights but on condition that no one asks us why.'"

This seems to have been an unavoidable condition for the Declaration, given what the signatories desired, and some may argue

70

that it still does not matter today. Expedient or aspirational as the Preamble's justifications are, they retain some power even if they don't have authority. Nevertheless, this is still an unhappy condition for humanism to find itself in—having no solid reason why we are committed to the thing (human worth) that we are most committed to. Pragmatic foundations are inherently vulnerable and even if the moral edifice that is constructed above them is unlikely to collapse altogether, it is surely beholden on us to construct it as securely as possible. Hence the question about which ideology best supports humanist ideals.

5

Before we can put the case for Christianity as better grounds for human dignity, it is worth considering the concept of the "human" itself, a point to which T. S. Eliot referred in his second Babbitt essay.

> Humanism depends very heavily . . . upon the tergiversations of the word "human"; . . . If you remove from the word "human" all that the belief in the supernatural has given to man, you can view him finally as no more than an extremely clever, adaptable, and mischievous little animal.

The phrase "all that the belief in the supernatural has given to man" is somewhat opaque but Eliot's central point is clear: defining the human is difficult when all reference to transcendence—or, at the very least, to any perception of transcendence—is removed.

This is not, it should be observed, an exclusively "religious" argument. The evolutionary psychologist Robin Dunbar, coming from as different a position from Eliot as is possible, had made a similar point, in so doing elucidating Eliot's contention:

> As remarkable as our achievements in the arts and sciences may be, it is hard to escape the conclusion that religion is the one phenomenon in which we humans really are different in some qualitative sense from our ape cousins . . . We should not, in our haste, overlook the important role religion has played in human affairs, helping to bond communities and so enabling them to meet the challenges that the planet has thrown at them. Even today, its contribution to human psychological well-being is probably sufficient to raise serious questions about whether the human race could do without it.

This offers an entirely functional understanding of religion, in which it is a unique human endeavor but one that is evolutionarily driven and determined rather than in any way a response to reality. This (significant) difference notwithstanding, the same conclusion beckons: if you seek an idea of the human on which to ground ideas of human dignity and rights, discarding the ideas and practices associated with religion leaves the boundaries blurred. Without some concept of self-transcendence—not *agreement* about it but simply acknowledging the concept—it is hard to see why one should draw the lines of the human to exclude, say, higher primates.

6

If the category of human is neither obvious nor natural, ascribing dignity or worth to *each and every* individual who falls within that category is even less natural.

This is emphatically not to say that humans don't have great capacity for goodness, for solidarity, for hospitality, and for generosity: in short, for behaving with dignity and affirming the worth of others. Nor is it to claim that we direct those virtues solely toward kin and kith, to those to whom we are related, whom we know or whom we may get some advantage from. As Larissa MacFarquhar illustrates in her book *Strangers Drowning: Voyages to the Brink of Moral Extremity*, there are some humans whose sense of moral responsibility is all but incalculable and whose response is supremely self-sacrificial. What it is to say is that, however generous we *can* be, it is certainly not natural or obvious for humans to ascribe dignity and worth to *all* humans *everywhere, irrespective* of capacity or circumstance.

The most cursory reading of human history confirms this, and the West is certainly no different from anywhere else in this respect. And yet it was in the West, specifically through the intrusion of Christianity into the thought world of late antiquity, that this changed.

To understand this it is important first to ask what it means to say that something has worth. The instinctive response to this is to seek the answer in a particular capacity or quality or function of the thing under discussion. A house has worth because of its size, style, and location; a car because of its design and performance; and so on. However, it soon becomes clear that this is a limiting approach. A child's teddy bear, for example, may be badly made, torn and battered beyond all recognition, incapable of *doing* anything and with no "functionality," and yet have immense and incommensurable worth. A love letter or family photograph may be similarly damaged and scruffy but have a similar value. By contrast, a brand-new consumer product may have highly impressive functionality but be so cosmetically damaged as to make it worthless. The properties or capacities of an object are no sure guide to its worth.

An alternative view is that something has worth on account of its scarcity. This seems instinctively correct, despite being wittily satirized in Thomas More's *Utopia*, whose inhabitants value things in proportion to their usefulness (e.g., iron) as opposed to their scarcity (e.g., gold). More's Utopians excepted, people do accord something worth in inverse proportion to its scarcity. However, this is no better a guide to worth than faculties or capacities.

It is certainly true that the price of gold rises or falls according to its availability (among other factors), but this indicates nothing more than the fact that people do value rare things; not that rarity itself is inherently valuable. The *Codex Sinaiticus* and the Lindisfarne Gospels are unique manuscripts and of enormous value. However, the early drafts of this book and the dumped rubbish at the end of my road are both similarly unique but they are pretty much worthless. A thing is not necessarily valuable simply because it is scarce or even unique.

The criterion for the worth of a thing is not, therefore, what it can do, what it looks like, or how many of them there are in existence. Rather, the primary criterion for worth is simply whether someone values it. The child's teddy bear, the love letter, and the family photograph have value because the child, lover, or mother is profoundly attached to them. The *Codex Sinaiticus* and the Lindisfarne Gospels have similar worth because scholars (and Christians) around the world value them for what they reveal about early Christianity. The damaged iPhone 5 or the dumped rubbish are all but worthless because no one values them. Disconcerting and relativistic as it may seem, the worth of something is dependent on the judgement of a person.

There is, of course, a difference between worth and dignity. A thing may have worth but it makes no sense to say that it has dignity. Dignity is an epithet we attach only to humans and the things they do.

However, to say that a human has dignity is to presuppose that he or she also has worth. It is this understanding of worth—someone has worth because he or she is valued by another—that lies at the heart of the Christian understanding of human dignity, the "another" in this context being, of course, God.

7

The biblical foundations of human dignity are well known, and although there are a number that might be cited, one in particular stands out: the idea that humans are made in the image of God.

There have been innumerable attempts to define what being made in the image of God "means," some more successful than others. For a time in the post-Reformation period, rationality was deemed to be *the* distinctive and decisive human capacity and therefore the mark of God's image. This had little textual warrant, however, and is largely discarded by theologians today. In its place a number of other definitions and characteristics stand out.

First, there is the "substantive" definition: being made in the image of God means sharing some of his substantial characteristics, not so much rationality as creativity, productivity, and generosity. The God in whose image humans are made is a creative, productive, and generous God. Second, there is the "functional" definition: being made in the image of God means we have a particular job to do, a job that is variously defined as "ruling over," "subdu[ing]," "work[ing] . . . and tak[ing] care of" and "nam[ing]" creation, or alternatively "stewardship." Finally, there is the relational definition: being made in the image of God means existing in relationship to him, to other humans, and to the rest of creation in a way that reflects something of God's own relational nature.

These are all defensible definitions but demand careful handling. They outline, in effect, a normative picture of the human in the sense of what humans *should ideally be like*, not what they *are* like. Our humanity may be distinguished by and aspire to this picture, but it consistently fails to achieve it. Recognizing this is important. Were we to predicate human worth on such nature, behavior, or capacities (on our relationality, our productivity, our generosity, etc.), our consistent failure to live up to these standards would erode that worth. In short, it would be a way of showing not human worth but worthlessness.

This is not, however, how Christian Scripture and thought does describe human worth. Indeed, the biblical understanding of the image of God is not interested in parsing the term, still less judging human worth by the extent to which we fulfil its constituent elements. Humans are not creatures that are valued by God because they bear the *imago dei*. Humans are creatures that bear the *imago dei* because they are valued by God.

This has obvious implications for how we should treat one another. Every person is made in the image of God; made in order to be in relationship, to be loving, creative, generous, and so forth. Every person fails in this commission. Some fail through ignorance, some through weakness, some through their own deliberate fault, hence Paul's judgement that all have sinned and fallen short of the glory of God: not the self-flagellating miserabilism of caricature but a recognition that all of us fail to be as loving and faithful, forgiving and forbearing, gentle and generous as we should; that we don't live up to the image of God.

However, our worth is not contingent on our doing so. Human worth is dependent not on how loving we are but how loved we are. In the long run it appears that the image of the child's battered teddy bear, while misleading in so many small ways, is right in one big one: it is not our capacities or beauty or lack thereof that matter; it is how much we are loved.

This is profoundly important for how we treat one another. For if all the above is true, whenever I interact with another creature that bears the image of God, I am interacting with someone who is loved fully and permanently by God. Their capacities and moral qualities, while being relevant to their role in society, have no bearing on their worth, which is determined by God alone.

This helps explain why the incursion of Christian ethical commitments into the ancient world was so strange, even incomprehensible, to so many. Early Christians repeatedly drew attention to the universality and impartiality of God's—and in theory therefore their—love. "Persons of every age are treated by us with respect . . . We do not test them by their looks, nor do we judge of those who come to us by their outward appearance," explained the Syrian writer Tatian.

Words are one thing, of course; actions another, and there was inevitably more than a touch of polemic to some Christian claims. The Church's funds are not "spent on feasts, and drinking bouts, and eating houses" (unlike those of pagan religions), explained the theologian Tertullian. Instead, they were used "to support and bury poor people, to supply the wants of boys and girls destitute of means and parents, and of old persons confined to the house." Yet this activity is too widely testified, not least by those who were Christianity's enemies, to be incredible. When the last pagan emperor, Julian the Apostate, complained how "the impious Galileans" (as he called them) "support our poor in addition to their own," he confirmed what Tertullian, and others, claimed.

The clearest mark of the early Church's humanism was found not just in its support of the pagan poor but also in the attention and respect it paid to those on the very margins of life. The Church, for example, inherited the—to the ancient world unfathomable—Jewish prohibition on abortion and infanticide. Its attitude to that other group of marginal humans, slaves, was more ambiguous, but only slightly more so. Because slavery in the ancient world ranged from comfortable domestic employment to brutal enslavement, the initial Christian response was to ameliorate rather than abolish. The very fact that slaves and masters shared the same body of Christ in the Eucharist slowly undermined the inherent inequality of the master–slave relationship, however. In time this would underpin Gregory of Nyssa's unequivocal and indignant denunciation of slavery in his fourth sermon on the book of Ecclesiastes in 379 and, eventually, lead to the erosion of the institution in later centuries.

Such attitudes to the poor, the unborn, the newborn, and slaves were eccentric. More directly challenging was the Christian attitude to taking life. Christians exhibited a distinct reluctance to take human lives. They denounced the public exhibition of the arena and rejected even authorized killing of an army. No Christian served in imperial armies until about AD 170, and even afterwards doing so was treated with great suspicion.

Altogether, for all its undoubted hesitations and failures (not that modern Western Christian authors are in any position to cast stones), the early Christian Church exhibited a deep and empire-transforming ideological and practical commitment to the dignity and worth of the human, a powerful and determined humanism, which may have been repeatedly betrayed in the time of Christendom but was never altogether lost.

8

It is this commitment to human dignity that still underpins humanism today. The human being is of worth irrespective of his or her standing in society, employment, or any other cultural norms.

However, this is the juncture at which the vulnerability of non-Christian humanist commitment to ineradicable human dignity becomes clear, for the simple fact that the foundational reason behind the Christian humanist commitment to human dignity is not available to atheists. Quite clearly it makes no sense for an atheist to say that God loves all those who bear his image, irrespective of whether they or anyone else erases, or even acknowledges, that image. The non-Christian humanist commitment to ineradicable human dignity must rely on some other factors, and none of these is quite up to the job.

Two stand out. Best known is the argument from capacities associated with Immanuel Kant. The argument here is that humans (uniquely) have the capacity for rational agency, and it is this capacity to direct their will to their own freely chosen ends that means "man exists as an end in himself, [and] not merely as a means for arbitrary use by this or that will." Since it is rational nature that makes you a person, it is in respecting that nature in you that another pays proper respect to you.

This sounds reasonable and humane but it is beset with problems, most notably: What of those human beings who do not have rational capacity? Do they therefore not have worth or dignity? In some instances the basic criterion of "rational capacity" can be massaged to accommodate them. Infants, for example, do not have rational capacity, but so long as human dignity is deemed to rest not on possession of rationality but *potential* possession of rationality, it can be argued that they do in fact have dignity and worth.

But this argument does not work for those with permanent mental illness or with degenerative conditions, like Alzheimer's or dementia, who have either never possessed such rationality or have lost it and have no chance of acquiring it again. In these instances there is no potential possession of rationality and so, presumably therefore, no dignity and worth.

The second response to the need for non-theistic foundations for human dignity is to assert that one does not need any allegedly external or objective basis, such as being loved by God or having rational faculties, in order to recognize human dignity. Rather, simply believing that humans have dignity is enough. This is the idea of the "useful myth," the commitment to which, if sufficiently widely held, becomes as close to being an objective fact as is possible for humans to achieve in such circumstances. This may sound absurd—a hauling oneself up by one's ethical bootstraps—but it is effectively the means by which the Universal Declaration of Human Rights has existed over the last sixty-five years ("We agree about the rights but on condition that no one asks us why"), the success of which has been far from negligible.

However, the example of the Universal Declaration illustrates precisely the problem with this approach. Put simply, it works when it works. In countries and cultures that sign up to and mentally internalize the Declaration, it retains a genuine power that becomes, in effect, authority. However, in times and places that fail to recognize let alone internalize the ideas, it has no hold. It is, in effect, a kind of faith. If held with sufficient strength and confidence it can discipline other less benevolent attitudes to the human. If not, it has no power at all.

It is perhaps for this reason that adherents of human rights sometimes attack its critics with such vigor. On this understanding, to criticize human rights is not to disagree about a political structure or even an ethical system, but to risk revealing the subjective basis of the whole system, to show that its foundation is no stronger than a silent, collective act of will. It is the equivalent of the Reformers casting doubts on what the priest accomplishes during Mass.

Thus while this approach *can* ground humanism's commitment to equal and inalienable human dignity, it depends on everyone believing in it, a colossal act of communal faith. This has worked well enough in the Western world for the last two generations but its success beyond these—historically Christian—countries has been far less impressive.

It is clearly too philosophically vulnerable an approach to sustain this commitment in the long run.

9

It is important to be clear about the argument being made here. This chapter does not contend that atheist humanists necessarily have any less commitment to human dignity than Christian humanists. Nor, obviously, has it claimed that they are less moral than Christians. What it *has* argued is that the Christian foundation for the human "dignity" or "worth" inherent within humanism is more robust than comparable atheistic foundations, and that without it, humanism's commitment to human dignity is weaker and perhaps even ultimately unsustainable.

To claim this is not, I hope, to be unduly apocalyptic, still less to criticize humanism, but rather, in the spirit of T. S. Eliot in 1928, merely "to point out the weak points in its defences, before some genuine enemy took advantage of them."

6

Christianity and Atheism: A Family Affair

———•◦•———

1

In 2007, Nicholas Lash, formerly Professor of Divinity at Cambridge University, wrote an article entitled "Where Does *The God Delusion* Come From?" He sought, first, to examine some of the book's chief weaknesses and, second, "to address the question of what it is about the climate of the times that enables so ill-informed and badly argued a tirade to be widely welcomed by many apparently well-educated people."

Lash offered a number of subtle and persuasive reasons but curiously omitted the single, most obvious one: when the book was published. *The God Delusion* hit the shelves in October 2006. That was six years into the Republican presidency of George W. Bush, an evangelical Christian who allegedly claimed that God wanted him to be president and who had come to power by drawing heavily on the support of the so-called Christian Right. It was five years after 9/11. It was three years into an enormously divisive invasion of Iraq, British participation in which was largely determined by the convictions of another publicly Christian political leader. It was a year after 7/7. It was a year or so after the nuclear program of the Islamic Republic of Iran had first become a serious international concern. And it was a year or so after the Islamist group Hamas had unexpectedly won the Palestinian elections. All in all, 2006 was not an auspicious moment in world history for religion, let alone for the interface of religion and politics.

If you want a reason why *The God Delusion* was so popular it is surely this. The book tapped into a very wide and very deep concern about the role of religion in the world today and, in particular, the role that religion threatens to play as soon as it gets anywhere near the levers of political power.

The same goes, on a slightly grander scale, for the whole New Atheist phenomenon. Although the term "New Atheism" was first coined, at least in the modern context, in 2006, the phenomenon is usually dated to the publication of Sam Harris's book *The End of Faith* in 2004, whose inspiration was confessedly "Islamic." Harris, beginning his book on 10/11, explained frankly that "we are at war with Islam . . . [not] with an otherwise peaceful religion that had been 'hijacked' by extremists . . . [but] with precisely the vision of life that is prescribed to all Muslims in the Koran."

New Atheism was not simply an anti-Islamic phenomenon. Christopher Hitchens enthusiastically opined that religion poisons "everything," and Richard Dawkins spent considerable time and energy in his own atheistic opus demolishing Christian beliefs. The New Atheists detested religion, not only Islam.

For all their prominence, the so-called four horsemen did not speak for all atheists, however, as some fellow travellers were keen to point out. In August 2013, the editor of *New Humanist*, the magazine of the Rationalist Association in Britain, wrote a piece claiming that Dawkins provided "a case study in how not to do it." He went on to point out that blanket condemnations of religious groups were morally dubious (as well as counterproductive); that religious believers were in fact no less intelligent than non-believers; and that secularism did not mean excluding religious believers from public life. Nor were all atheistic views that broke cover during this period as relentlessly negative as those of the New Atheists. As noted in the previous chapter, recent years have witnessed a highly articulate group of atheists try to capture "humanism" as the exclusive vehicle for their non-religious beliefs. New Atheism should not be confused with all atheism.

Nevertheless, such caveats recognized, the New Atheists' focus on and fury with religion is telling and significant, not least as it offers a key to understanding the history of atheism and, in particular, how much it owes to Christianity.

2

Despite having a very rich vocabulary for heresy, the European middle ages had no word for atheism. The Christian culture of the day was simply too thick, too total for people to identify, name, or even grasp such thoroughgoing unbelief.

That didn't, of course, mean there was no unbelief. The heresy registers of Bishop Fournier of Pamiers in the early fourteenth century include accusations of religious skepticism, materialism, and disbelief in the afterlife. Thomas Semer, or Taylor, accused of Lollardy in the mid-fifteenth century, appears to have been a more comprehensive doubter, denying the existence of the soul, of heaven, hell, and purgatory, claiming that Christ was nothing but a man born of Joseph and Mary and that the Eucharist was nothing more than bread.

However skeptical such views were, they were still understood as (extreme) variations of Christianity. For atheism to become a recognized entity in itself, as opposed to a greater or lesser deviation from Christian orthodoxy, the Christian culture in which it grew needed to be broken up and the thick, coherent Christian world view to come apart. This is precisely what happened in the sixteenth century, which was also the period in which the term "atheist" was coined in European vernacular languages. It occurred in four ways.

First, the ancient world was rediscovered. Classical texts had, of course, been emerging for centuries in Europe, and it was the "rediscovery" of Aristotle in the twelfth century that had helped precipitate Europe's first—or second, if you count the Carolingian—Renaissance. In spite of some ecclesiastical hostility, classical ideas were rapidly and usually comfortably integrated within the Christian world view. Humanist scholars may have been treated with some suspicion, but they were, as a rule, devout, if unusually broad-minded, Christians.

Such integration became more challenging in the 1500s, however, when some ideas, like Pyrrhonian skepticism, and some texts, like Lucretius's poem *On the Nature of Things*, became public. Pyrrhonian skepticism argued that humans could never be sure whether reliable knowledge was possible, and so should withhold judgement on all questions. A number of Christian thinkers approved of this turn, as they took it to mean that, not being able to trust the evidence of mind or senses, humans should rely on the revelation of Scripture or the Church's magisterium if they wanted certainty. Skepticism nevertheless still left an uncomfortable taste in the mind. "The Holy Ghost is not a Skeptic," Luther wrote contemptuously to Erasmus.

Harder still to reconcile was Lucretius's *De rerum natura*, a 7,000-line poem that showcased a view of the world that was made up of atoms, chance, and distant, disinterested gods, with no creator, no designer, and no plan. This view was utterly different from the conventional Christian one, and one that was, in effect, wholly incompatible. It is questionable whether anyone lost their faith on account of Pyrrho or Lucretius, but their thought did open up disturbing new ways of seeing the world.

Lucretius's new world was a metaphorical one, but at the same time more literal, foreign "worlds" were opening up the European imagination. This was the second way in which the coherent medieval Christian world view came apart. Increased presence and trade in Southern and Eastern Asia alerted Western Europeans to cultures and traditions of scholarship that were ancient—perhaps more ancient than those of the Mediterranean—and which had ideas of God that were hard to square with those of Christendom. The New World too offered its challenges, less on account of the primitive cultures found there (which were judged simply to be in need of Christian civilization), and more because they were apparently unknown to that source of all reliable knowledge, the Bible.

This in itself was hardly a killer blow (indeed, it is arguable that respect for the ancients was more eroded by this apparent lacuna in geographical knowledge than was the Bible). New worlds could, however, provide a different kind of provocation, with reports and stories from foreign lands raising awkward questions about pleasure, ethics, and moral relativism. They seemed to show that there were many different ways of living in the world, each with its own particular intellectual, moral, and spiritual dimensions and—crucially—that whichever one adopted was due simply to the accident of one's birth. In the words of the once respected, but increasingly suspected, preacher and theologian, Pierre Charron, "one's nation, one's country, one's home determines one's religion . . . We are circumcised or baptized—Jews, or Muslims, or Christians—before we know we are human beings. It is not we who choose our religions." This was ominous enough, but it became still more so when some self-evidently sophisticated cultures, such as that encountered by missionaries in China, appeared to have no concept of God at all, thereby undermining the idea that there was a *sensus divinitatis* that all possessed.

A third, less tangible but still more threatening, new world that opened up was the appalling inner one associated with Niccolo Machiavelli. Machiavelli's inadvisably honest tract on statecraft, *The Prince*, originally written to curry favor with Lorenzo de' Medici, revealed not only breathtaking cynicism but, more alarmingly, a vision of the world in which might was right, a prospect that terrified contemporaries perhaps because it was so credible. The ethical strings that bound the society together and prevented every village, every church, every kingdom from degenerating into an anarchy of self-interest and power were slashed through. As far as *The Prince* was concerned, the theological cure was no better than the sinful poison. Machiavelli's world was brutal and amoral. Religion was a tool of political control. God was, for all intents and purposes, absent. The law was, at best, a temporary, expedient measure. What mattered was survival and power. Machiavelli himself became a shorthand for feigned piety, amorality, cynicism, political violence, and, naturally, godlessness. This was the vision of an atheistic world that no one sought, but the sheer, realistic vividness of Machiavelli's depiction meant that few could dismiss it either.

The fourth and, of course, biggest breakdown in the Christian world view was the confessional split that scythed through Europe in the sixteenth and seventeenth centuries. This had several impacts on the emergence of atheism, foremost among them being a massive epistemic crisis: how, now, were people to know the truth of the world, of the cosmos, of God, of themselves? The answer, at first, was still the Bible, but the questions persisted: which Bible and whose interpretation?

Protestants claimed that the Vulgate, the fourth-century Latin translation that had long been authoritative within the Church, was error-strewn. The Catholic response was that the original Hebrew text, on which St. Jerome had drawn for his translation and which was now lost, had been superior to the current Hebrew text, which had been corrupted over the centuries. Questions of textual reliability, compositional process, and authorship thus became weapons in the confessional battles of the time, each side seeking to undermine the foundation of the other's faith.

More urgent than the question of which text was whose interpretation. Was it, as some Reformers claimed (at least at first), the individual's, albeit tutored by the Holy Spirit? If so, how was one to judge between the wildly different views that emerged whenever power and censorship broke down? Was it, conversely, the teaching of the Church? If so, how did one deal with the ecclesiastical corruption that was evident to so many? Was it perhaps church tradition? If so, who was to say the Church Fathers were infallible in their interpretation of Scripture?

Confessional blocs emerged across Europe along the famous formula of *Cuius regio eius religio*—"whose realm, his religion"—and the Bible was caught in the crossfire, damaged in the process. Not surprisingly, in the aftermath of Europe's (first) civil war, theologians turned to non-confessional sources, in particular the natural world, as the basis for their knowledge, while atheist polemicists drew on these confessional tactics for their wholesale attack on Christianity.

Much more serious than even this, however, was the bloodshed that marked these disputes. Confessional lines didn't directly translate into military ones but doctrinal disputes nonetheless became bloodily entangled with political ones. When debunking the scale of early Christian martyrdom in his *Decline and Fall* in the 1780s, Edward Gibbon pointedly remarked that "Christians, in the course of their intestine dissensions, have inflicted far greater severities on each other, than they had experienced from the zeal of infidels." Indeed, he continued, if we are to believe Grotius, "the number of Protestants, who were executed in a single province and a single reign, far exceeded that of the primitive martyrs in the space of three centuries, and of the Roman empire." The point was clear: Christian society was itself far more bloody and oppressive than the pagan world it had allegedly conquered in peace. This became key to atheism's future. Atheism was not simply a legitimate world view, newly emerged from the cracks of Christendom, but an alternative, an *appealing* alternative, a reaction against the bloody womb from which it had emerged.

3

This tension—between being something new and something reactive—became central to the subsequent history of atheism. The desire to offer a genuinely new and different vision of reality meant that atheism had to be more than just a statement about the nonexistence of God. Rather, it was also a statement about the nature of humanity, of society, of the world, in the light of God's nonexistence. It had, in effect, to be a viable alternative to Christianity, but that invariably meant it adopted from and responded to the (kinds of) Christianity in which it emerged.

This helps to explain why atheism took different forms in different cultures. England, latterly Britain, experienced considerable intellectual toleration in the later seventeenth and eighteenth centuries. The 1663 Charter of the pioneering Royal Society declared that the Society's activities shall be devoted "to the glory of God the Creator," and its officers were required to swear an oath on the Gospels. Robert Boyle, one of the greatest scientists of the age, died in 1691 and in his will left funds for a lecture series intended "for the defense of the Christian religion against atheists and other unbelievers." The first lecturer, Richard Bentley, spoke on the *Confutation of Atheism* and was himself a protégé of Isaac Newton, one of the few scholars who outshone Boyle and who was vocal in his belief that his work supported and glorified God. Indeed, Bentley, seeking his master's help for his inaugural lecture, received four detailed letters from him, the first of which began:

> when I wrote my treatise about our System I had an eye upon such Principles as might work with considering men for the belief of a Deity & nothing can rejoice me more then to find it useful for that purpose.

It was a similar story politically and ecclesiastically. In the last decade of the seventeenth century, England became a beacon of religious toleration, of limited and accountable government, and of economic stability. This was justified on theological grounds, supremely in the work of John Locke, whose first *Letter Concerning Toleration* and *First Treatise on Government* were not only widely read and hugely respected but also clearly and explicitly biblical in their reasoning.

None of this meant there were no doubters. A "deist scare," which began in the 1690s, produced some of Europe's earliest prominent skeptics, such as Antony Collins, Matthew Tindal, John Toland, and Thomas Woolston. More famously, mid-eighteenth-century Britain produced two of Europe's most sophisticated skeptics, David Hume and Edward Gibbon. None of these doubting luminaries ever matured into full-scale atheists, however, in large measure because the Christian culture in which they operated made it very difficult for them to. When Robert Boyle and Isaac Newton claimed that "science" produced manifold evidences of God's power and goodness, and when John Locke advocated an almost unprecedentedly liberal and tolerant political system on theological grounds, it was a brave man who could confidently declare otherwise.

Things were different in France. Louis XIV became ever more intolerant and pious in the later years of his reign, revoking the Edict of Nantes, which had guaranteed French Protestants a measure of security, and banning many of the entertainments he had previously enjoyed. He forbade the teaching of Cartesianism in French colleges and universities, enforcing an (already outmoded) Aristotelianism which was, in any case, kept thoroughly subordinate to theology. The French Church was gloriously wealthy, owning close to 10 percent of land, exercising the right to tithe over most of the rest, and enjoying significant tax exemptions while all the time nourishing popular hostility to Protestants. French nobles, officials, and diplomats hardly bothered to conceal their freethinking, libertine views while the state maintained the strictest oppression of unorthodoxy. Whereas most of its neighbors symbolically tore or burnt books, or imprisoned their authors, France still allowed torture and execution for confessional crimes, and as late as 1766, Chevalier de la Barre was publicly tortured for reputedly singing blasphemous songs, disrespecting a religious procession, and owning a copy of Voltaire's *Philosophical Dictionary*.

It was in this context that Europe's first confirmed atheists emerged, and they were every bit as angry as their twenty-first-century descendants. The first of whom we can say that he was definitely an atheist was Jean Meslier, who was born in 1664, took Holy Orders in January 1689, and thereafter lived an unremarkable clerical life but whose posthumously discovered *Memoire* made *The God Delusion* seem like a sober and balanced piece of scholarship. Meslier had minimal influence as an atheist as his work was popularized by the deistic Voltaire, who feared and detested atheists almost as much as his Catholic foes and who accordingly castrated Meslier's book, turning it into an anticlerical rather than atheistic tract.

More influential were the great and good who gathered round the dining table of Paul-Henri Thiry, Baron d'Holbach in Paris in the 1750s and '60s. Holbach was known as the personal enemy of God. By his measure, religion was simply the result of superstition and ignorance, accepted through custom alone and defenceless against serious thought. Faith was the opposite to reason, repeatedly described as a form of blindness that demanded the wholesale abandonment of common sense and submission to corrupt ecclesiastical authorities. Faith demeaned and degraded. Man made gods, which were merely personifications of nature, and religions altered them according to their needs.

These were views shared by many mid-century French skeptics, most of whom were his dinner guests. Some like Denis Diderot slid almost unwillingly from deism to materialism. Others like Claude Adrien Helvétius were more interested in the potential that godlessness gave to human conditioning through education. Still others, like Julien Offray de La Mettrie, who was not one of Holbach's guests, argued on scientific grounds that all mental activity was merely an aspect of physical activity, and that therefore, with no afterlife to aspire to or no immortal soul to protect, humans should only live for the pleasure of the present. The great mid-century French atheists thus held subtly different atheistic world views, which would emerge in similar forms in different countries over the next two centuries. What united and inspired them was the intellectually and politically narrow, hypocritical, oppressive, and often viciously brutal Christian culture in which they lived, one that, failing to bend, finally snapped in 1789.

One further example from the eighteenth century should underline the significance of Christianity to the emergence of atheism. The

United States became the West's most self-consciously modern nation. If modernity were obviously correlated with atheism, then America should also be its most atheistic. But atheism never really happened to the United States. In the first instance, many American clergy enthusiastically supported the Revolution, describing it as a just war. Christianity in America became associated with the people's political emancipation, in a way that it did only partially in Britain and not at all in France.

This association was supplemented with what, in all honesty, were some pretty unpersuasive myths about the faith of the Founding Fathers (a still lively topic in the US culture wars). While some, such as John Witherspoon, a signatory of the Declaration of Independence, John Jay, the first Chief Justice, and Samuel Adams were orthodox in their faith, the more prominent, such as Thomas Jefferson and Benjamin Franklin, were certainly not, being vague deists with an interest in Christ's moral teachings, while George Washington himself was reticent about his beliefs, albeit convinced that God could and did intervene in human affairs. Such a sense of providence was to pervade the identity of the new nation, making wholesale atheism, if not impossible, then at least more difficult.

It was the fact that public atheism wasn't legally impossible—as it effectively was in Europe—that was to become America's greatest insurance against it, however. The US Constitution did not refer to God (save for a reference to the Year of our Lord in Article VII), precluded any religious test from becoming a requirement for office and, most famously, in its first Amendment legislated against Congress making any law "respecting an establishment of religion, or prohibiting the free exercise thereof." In this way, not only did America simultaneously associate Christianity with the liberty achieved at the nation's foundation but it prevented clerics from getting their hands on power in such a way as to dirty this reputation. Atheism, in effect, had little to go on.

4

The final and full emergence of atheism in the nineteenth and twentieth centuries offers up a much bigger picture about which it is, naturally, harder to generalize. Nevertheless, the essential outline—of the necessary and sometimes parasitic relationship with Christianity—remains visible. We can see this in the examples of Britain, France, Germany, and Russia.

The British reaction to the French Revolution at first cemented Christianity as part of national life, something neatly exemplified by the *Encyclopaedia Britannica*. This was first conceived as a riposte to the more famous French *Encyclopédie*. By the turn of the century it was in its third edition, to which was added a supplement in which the editors wrote, in dedication to the king:

> The French *Encyclopédie* has been accused, and justly accused, of having disseminated far and wide the seeds of anarchy and atheism. If the *Encyclopaedia Britannica* shall in any degree counteract the tendency of that pestiferous work, even these two volumes will not be wholly unworthy of your Majesty's patronage.

Christian British encyclopaedias thus went to war with atheist French ones.

In the years after the Napoleonic wars, the country passed increasingly repressive laws, usually defended by the same Anglican aristocracy that had fought for the abolition of slavery. Simultaneously, it industrialized along the lines of an unforgiving political economy, justified and legitimized by prominent clerical thinkers such as Thomas Malthus and John Bird Sumner, latterly archbishop of Canterbury.

The result of these two social upheavals was the first stirrings of public atheism in Britain, primarily as a working-class movement, among figures like Richard Carlile and George Jacob Holyoake. Even here, however, the presence of long-tolerated dissenting groups in emerging cities meant that the greatest working-class movement of the period, Chartism, never attained the atheistic momentum it might have done (and that similar movements did on the Continent). Indeed, Chartism was, in the words of historian Michael Burleigh, "little more than a secularised form of Methodism."

If economically British Christianity drew British atheism's teeth, the manner in which the British *ancien régime* was unpicked from 1828 onwards further de-fanged the movement. The historian Owen Chadwick once remarked that "the old Christian state was dismantled by Christians for the sake of keeping the people Christian." It worked. Chadwick went on to remark that the 1880s was the closest Britain ever came to seeing the working classes going secular, not for any new philosophical reasons, still less Darwinian ones, but because the early part of the decade witnessed the confluence of an economic downturn and the scandal of the nation's first openly atheist MP, Charles Bradlaugh, being denied his seat in Parliament. Ultimately, the economy recovered, Bradlaugh was allowed to take his seat, and the nascent British atheist movement faded. As one secular leader observed at the time, the British people seemed to sense that secular societies were like Turkish baths: good to pass through but not to live in.

The French experience of atheism in the nineteenth century also grew under the shadow of the French Revolution, although in a different way from the British. Post-Napoleonic France was caught between skeptical rationalism—felt to be shallow, desiccated, desolating—and the old religious regime, which in spite of a resurgent and triumphant Catholicism, could not simply resume the territory it had lost in the 1790s. Forced to choose between the unpalatable and incredible, a bewildering range of "spiritual" beliefs and practices flourished, while some creative thinkers invented a wholesale new religion. Henri de Saint-Simon and, in his footsteps, Auguste Comte developed a *Nouveau Christianisme* and a Religion of Humanity, also known as Positivism. This aped Christian theology (and numerology), positing a three-stage process—religious, metaphysical, and finally scientific—through which society passed as knowledge became more assured. It developed a series of elaborate rituals, which Positivists were mandated to obey. Thus the faithful Positivist was to pray three times a day (once to each of his household goddesses: mother, wife, and daughter); to cross himself by tapping his head with his finger three times in the place where, according to phrenology, the impulses of benevolence, order, and progress were to be found; and to proceed through nine sacraments, beginning with presentation (a form of baptism) and proceeding to initiation, admission, destination, marriage (at a specified age), maturity, retirement, transformation, and then, seven years after death, incorporation. T. H. Huxley, Darwin's famous bulldog, later described Positivism as "Catholicism minus Christianity." The criticism was both withering and accurate: once again atheism was profoundly molded by its Christian culture, albeit less violently than had been the case in the previous century.

Germany took a path closer to eighteenth- than nineteenth-century France. The preeminent philosopher of the early years of the century, Georg Hegel, felt, like some of his more eccentric French counterparts, that he too had moved beyond the anti-Christian polemic of the Enlightenment *philosophes* without abandoning Christianity's kernel. His articulation of the idea of the Spirit—of a nation, of an age, ultimately of the world—envisaged (or at least assumed) progress, albeit punctuated with repeated, necessary conflicts.

Such ideas were developed by a group of disciples, known as Young or Left Hegelians, who began their academic life in the master's slipstream but, somewhat less inclined to embrace Christianity with their master's lofty condescension, went their own radical ways from the 1830s. At that time, two out of every five graduates from German universities studied theology. The number of ecclesiastical positions available was inadequate to this supply, however, and those that were available were open only to graduates of conservative theological and political opinion, or who were from the aristocracy. With political pamphleteering forbidden, theology came to serve as a substitute for radical discourse and there emerged a kind of "intellectual proletariat," theologically literate, ecclesiastically alienated, and disaffected with the civil and religious establishment. So it was that the Young Hegelians, among them Ludwig Feuerbach (author of *The Essence of Christianity*), David Strauss (*The Life of Jesus, Critically Examined*), Bruno Bauer, Karl Marx, and Friedrich Engels articulated a theologically and philosophically sophisticated and politically animated atheism that was unique at the time and would come, through Marx's work, to reshape the world.

Russia gives a final example of how Christianity shaped the particular national contours of atheism. Because God was the basis of all hierarchy in Russia, whether moral, political, or epistemological, and because that hierarchy was so aggressively enforced, Russian atheism took upon itself a moral and political anger that was akin to that of the French *philosophes*. In the middle years of the century, thinkers like Alexander Herzen, and his friend the poet Nikolai Ogarev, influenced by Hegel and by intellectual trends in France, adopted a straightforwardly reformist message, advocating a return to the simplicity of the gospel and away from the corrupting accretions of Orthodoxy. Even this, however, was deemed a threat. Attitudes hardened and the next generation were more Young Hegelian than Hegelian in their objectives.

At the same time as these atheistic ideas were making inroads among the Russian intelligentsia, the aged Nicholas I was grappling with the slow industrialization and urbanization of his country. The Europe-wide revolutions of 1848 induced panic at home and confirmed the dangers inherent in Westernization. Archimandrite Ignatius Brianchaninov blamed revolutions on "rationalism" and demanded an immediate religious response. Censorship, hardly lax, was tightened, plots discovered, and plotters executed or exiled to hard labor in Siberia.

This combination of theo-political oppression and the assertion of human autonomy and progress gave early Russian atheism an anger unmatched even in France. Following Nicholas I's death in 1855, and amid the ongoing humiliation of the Crimean War, his son Alexander II engaged in a program of military, administrative, and economic reform, including, most significantly, the emancipation of Russia's 20 million or so peasants. This helped ease tension but was too little too late for Russia's atheistic radicals, who saw the act as mere palliation, its terms insufficiently generous and its processes unduly brutal.

By the end of the century, Russia was one of the few major European powers that remained not only almost entirely devoid of political liberal ideals but willing to impose the theologically sustained political autocracy by violence. On Sunday, January 9, 1905, Father Georgy Gapon marched at the head of 150,000 hymn-singing workers to submit a Humble and Loyal Petition to the Tsar at the Winter Palace in St. Petersburg. Imperial soldiers blocked their way and fired two warning volleys into the air. The workers continued to advance. The soldiers fired on the crowd and charged. Two hundred workers were killed, many more wounded.

Father Gapon survived. "There is no God any longer," he later said. "There is no Tsar."

5

Writing of the emergence of Russian atheism between the 1820s and 1860s, Victoria Frede observed that

> to treat atheism as a doctrine is . . . to miss its most salient feature. In Russia, it was less a statement about the status of God than it was a commentary on the status of educated people in an authoritarian state that sought ever more forcefully to regulate the opinions and beliefs of its subjects.

This applies just as much to Britain, Germany, France, or the USA as it does to Russia. Having been the womb in which Western atheism was conceived, Christianity then became its mother. In some countries it proved an errant and abusive parent, raising a child that was angry, hurt, aggressive, and sometimes violent. In others it was gentler, even indulgent, tolerating and even learning from its offspring's ideas and even, uniquely in the USA, limiting its own authority so that it became unable to inflict any lasting harm even in the supposed name of doing good.

So to return to where we started, we should not perhaps have been so surprised to see New Atheism emerge when it did, even in comparatively placid Britain, where books—novels indeed—had been burned on the streets in religious protest in a way that hadn't been seen for centuries. It would be unduly simplistic to say that Christianity was to blame for atheism, just as it would be unfair to say that atheism was only a reaction to, or parasite on, Christianity. But atheism's emergence in the modern West owes very much more to Christian thought and practice than atheists, or Christians, often realize.

7

The Accidental Midwife:
The Emergence of a Scientific Culture

1

In Part 3 of *Gulliver's Travels*, Lemuel Gulliver visits the Grand Academy of Lagado, the largest metropolis of Balnibarbi. The Academy, we are told, had its origins about forty years before Gulliver's visit when "certain persons" returned from Laputa, the island that floated above Balnibarbi, "with a very little smattering in mathematics, but full of volatile spirits acquired in that airy region." Disliking the management of "everything below," they "fell into schemes of putting all arts, sciences, languages, and mechanics, upon a new foot" and procured a royal patent for erecting an academy of "projectors," by means of whom a vast panoply of projects was established as a way of improving on life and nature.

Gulliver is shown round the Academy in Book 5. There he meets one projector who "has been eight years upon a project for extracting sunbeams out of cucumbers . . . to warm the air in raw inclement summers." A second was engaged in an "operation to reduce human excrement to its original food." A third was learning how to plow fields by means of pigs and strategically placed acorns, while a fourth was working out how to get silk from spiders. A "most ingenious architect" was contriving a new method for building houses "by beginning at the roof, and working downward to the foundation," while a group of blind men were being taught to distinguish between colors of paint by feel and smell. Reflecting on the Academy's great ambitions in his matchlessly deadpan tone, Gulliver laments that "the only inconvenience is, that none of these projects are yet brought to perfection; and [that] in the mean time, the whole country lies miserably waste, the houses in ruins, and the people without food or clothes."

Swift's picture of the Grand Academy of Lagado still has the power to amuse today, even for those unaware he was satirizing the Royal Society, founded about forty years before Gulliver set off on his third voyage, and the subject of great honor and great mockery.

Although granted a Royal Charter in 1662, the Society, contrary to initial hopes and expectations, failed to secure a royal endowment and was dependent in its early years on fees and subscriptions. For all his royal support, Charles II still referred to the Fellows as "my ferrets," and laughed at them, as did many others, for spending their time trying to weigh air and the like. The English divine Thomas Sprat wrote a somewhat premature *History of the Royal Society* in 1667, recording and honoring the progress Fellows had "already made" in the hope that this "learned and inquisitive age . . . will think their endeavors worthy of its assistance." Many, however, did not. Thomas Shadwell's comedy *The Virtuoso* of 1676 ridiculed natural philosophers, in particular Robert Hooke as Sir Nicholas Gimcrack, "who has broken his brains about the nature of maggots" (there is a reason why we read Jonathan Swift today and not Thomas Shadwell).

The fact that the activities of these early scientists—the word itself was 170 years off being coined but may be used of this period without too much anachronism—were judged so self-evidently ridiculous is instructive. "Science"—its interests, its approach, its methods—was strange, counterintuitive at best, preposterous and absurd at worst. There was nothing natural, nothing self-evidently admirable, and certainly nothing inevitable about its success.

Historians have long asked why the Scientific Revolution happened, and why it happened when it did. Some, however, in particular the historian of ideas Stephen Gaukroger, have refined this question, on the basis that in actual fact plenty of cultures saw the emergence of the kind of thinking and approach that characterized the late sixteenth and seventeenth centuries in England (and elsewhere in Europe). Lots of places, in effect, had scientific revolutions. Classical Greece is the most obvious example, not only witnessing to the birth of philosophy but also science, Aristotle being the first genuine scientist in history, at least according to the *Encyclopaedia Britannica*. The Hellenic intellectual diaspora and its influence on Roman culture might count as a second example: although unburdened by any single figure of

Aristotle's stature, it could still boast Galen, Ptolemy, and Pliny's massive *Natural History*, thinkers who can lay claim to the longest period of scientific dominance in Western history, their theories still being judged authoritative well over a millennium later.

A third example would undoubtedly be the flowering Arab-Islamic science in the Near East from the ninth to thirteenth centuries, which, again building on the Hellenic science that was lost to the Western empire, saw work of enormous erudition and sophistication in mathematics, astronomy, and medicine, through the industry of thinkers like al-Battani, al-Razi, and, most famously (at least in Europe), Avicenna and Averroes.

A fourth and perhaps the most famous example is that of China, the world's leading civilization in technological and, arguably, scientific terms by the fourteenth century but one whose failure to capitalize on this and transform it into a full-scale "Scientific Revolution" so perplexed the British scientist and historian Joseph Needham that he began a series of volumes on science and civilization in China—the first of which was published in 1954—and now stands, twenty years after his death, at seven volumes published in twenty-seven books.

Given these impressive examples, the question is less why did "science" happen in sixteenth–seventeenth-century Europe than why did it continue happening there? Why was it that that which Swift so ruthlessly mocked did not simply conform to the pattern of previous scientific moments—sporadic, intermittent, movements of curiosity and practical implementation that were effectively just one interesting activity among many others, and failed to generate their intellectual legitimacy? Why, in short, did this particular and far from unprecedented scientific revolution become The Scientific Revolution?

2

There are various answers to this question. Some are fairy tales, *Just So* stories told round atheist campfires as a way of keeping warm, keeping together, and keeping the flame of reason burning against the encroaching darkness of irrationality that always threatens to overcome it. These are, in effect, that somehow in sixteenth–seventeenth-century Europe, science managed to free itself from the clutches of religion in a way that earlier scientific revolutions had done only imperfectly or not at all, thereby liberated to bear the torch of disinterested truth ever onwards and upwards. It is a tale that is true enough to be believable even if it's not true enough to be true. A credible theory in the later nineteenth century, when Pope Pius IX published his Syllabus of Errors (which notoriously concluded that the Pontiff ought not to "come to terms with progress, liberalism and modern civilization"); when the first Vatican Council dogmatically defined the long-standing doctrine that when the pope spoke *ex cathedra* in matters of faith and morals, he did so with Christ's gift of infallibility; and when historians of science published books like the *History of the Conflict between Religion and Science* (John William Draper) or *History of the Warfare of Science with Theology in Christendom* (Andrew Dickson White), this theory nonetheless fails to fit the historical facts and is not taken very seriously today.

Less egregious but no more convincing are a variety of ideas that explain science's particular success at this particular juncture of history by reference to its particular characteristics at that time and place. In this fashion, one argument is that early science combined an aversion to dogmatism with a *constructively* adversarial culture in such a way as maintained an open mind while genuinely advancing knowledge. Here, iron sharpened iron without fear of consequence.

Here again, however, the facts don't quite fit the theory. Not only could pioneer natural philosophers be as dogmatic as their less empirical predecessors, but in reality the Aristotelianism against which many rebelled was a much more adversarial discipline and judged helplessly sterile for being so. Bacon, Descartes, Boyle, and Hobbes all explicitly distanced selves from this kind of adversarial approach. This did not, of course, mean that early modern science was—or should be—free from dispute. Newton's unparalleled achievements, for example, were studded with ferocious quarrels with other scientific luminaries, such as Robert Hooke and Leibniz, who was memorably described by Newton's disciple Roger Cotes, in the preface to the second edition of *Principia Mathematica*, as a "miserable reptile." This was an informal and far from productive adversarial culture, however; a very long way from the image of graceful, swan-like progress that the principles of collaboration, experiment, review, and publication would earn science.

Another idea is that at this time the scientific method delivered demonstrable truth and/or tangible results in a way that previous scientific revolutions did not. This, alas, while sounding wonderful is even less convincing as a theory. Chinese "science" was palpably more practically successful than its early modern European counterpart, boasting porcelain, cast iron, the plowshare, the stirrup, gunpowder, paper, printing, ink, the magnetic compass, and clockwork mechanism among its achievements. Early modern Europeans certainly aspired to such glories—Bacon claimed that "the true and lawful goal of the sciences is none other than . . . that human life be endowed with new discoveries and powers"—but Swift's satire was so successful precisely because the early Fellows of the Royal Society had not yet delivered the practical goods. Moreover, tangible advances in science for the first hundred or so years after the Restoration were due less to the formal pursuit of such Fellows and more to the work of outsiders and "inspired amateurs." The Lunar Men of Birmingham rather than the Fellows of London were the engine of the Industrial Revolution.

A third, more sociologically grounded explanation for this moment of success in European natural philosophy lies in the presence and role of free institutions. Self-governing corporate entities or institutions, such as the Royal Society or, before it, the universities, offered legally protected space for disinterested investigation, of a kind that was notably absent in the Islamic and Chinese worlds. This story does at least have the merits of tracing the Scientific Revolution way back into its historical hinterland—indeed all the way back to the Investiture Crisis of the eleventh century and the subsequent development of medieval canon law—rather than imagining it to have been created in the historical equivalent of six days of frenetic semi-divine activity at some point in the mid-seventeenth century. It is, if you like, an evolutionary explanation for early modern science, rather than a creationist one.

The problem is, once again, that the evidence doesn't fit the thesis. As Stephen Gaukroger observes, "if there were any 'neutral spaces' in the first half of the seventeenth century . . . they were not much in evidence in universities." Most of the greatest scientific names of the age were not university men. Simon Stevin, Pierre Gassendi, Thomas Harriot, Kenelm Digby, Galileo, and Hobbes were all in positions of patronage; Descartes and Boyle had their own means; Bacon was in public employment. Early modern science was not a triumph of the academy. More pointedly, even had it been, that might have generated a fruitful explanation for its genesis, and not necessarily for its wider uptake and credibility, for the development of a scientific *culture*.

The problem then stands, all the more starkly for reasons of such failed explanations. Why did a scientific revolution become The Scientific Revolution? What generated the scientific culture of early modern Europe?

3

This is precisely the question that a number of recent historians of science have grappled with, Stephen Gaukroger and Peter Harrison supreme among them, and their answers have invariably led back to the Christian culture in which the Revolution occurred. In Gaukroger's words:

> a distinctive feature of the Scientific Revolution is that, unlike other scientific programmes and cultures, it is driven, often explicitly, by religious considerations: Christianity set the agenda for natural philosophy in many respects and projected it forward in a way quite different from that of any other scientific culture.

What should be made clear straightaway is that this was hardly an uncomplicated, uncontested, or even necessarily intentional process. If Christianity acted as the midwife to the Scientific Revolution and, through it, to the culture of science that marked modernity, it was often as an accidental midwife.

Dean Swift's lacerating satire is evidence enough that some clergy were firmly on the side of mockery and contempt, and his was hardly a lone voice. In a sermon preached in Westminster Abbey in the year Thomas Sprat published his adulatory history, the Public Orator of the University of Oxford, Robert South, denounced Fellows of the Royal Society as "the profane, atheistical, epicurean rabble . . . who have lived so much to the defiance of God."

Such theological hostility was hardly new to the Restoration. Gaukroger shows how naturalistic ideas emerged in the later fifteenth century, in particular in the University of Padua, where they derived from Averroist doctrines that adopted a material reading of Aristotle's ideas of the soul. They were judged deeply worrying by the orthodox. Thinkers like Pietro Pomponazzi and, later, Bernardino Talesio expanded the domain of natural philosophy, openly questioning the extent to which it needed any form of "supernatural" supplement, and showed a conspicuous lack of interest in reconciling it with Christian doctrine. This kind of natural philosophy as an autonomous discipline was indeed a threat, as the authorities recognized in the bluntest possible of ways in the case of science's first great martyr, Giordano Bruno, who took the ideas of scientific autonomy to extremes in the last years of the sixteenth century by advocating a radically "natural" world view, which exhibited little more than contempt for other forms of reasoning.

In truth, such resistance antedated even Bruno, Talesio, and Pomponazzi by centuries. Gaukroger begins his book *The Emergence of a Scientific Culture*, the first of a projected four volumes describing the development and consolidation of a scientific culture in the modern West, by discussing the medieval Church's resistance to Aristotle, beginning in 1210 when the University of Paris first formally banned all public and private teaching of Aristotle's natural philosophy under penalty of excommunication.

Indeed, to complete the retrospective tour of anti-"scientific" Christian views, you can (and Gaukroger's does) go back much earlier to find evidence of the Church Fathers' antipathy. Ambrose of Milan, for example, a major figure in his own right as well as being St. Augustine's mentor, wrote that "there is no place in the words of the Holy Scripture for the vanity of perishable knowledge which deceives and deludes us in our attempt to explain the unexplainable." A century and a half before him, Tertullian explained that "we have no need for curiosity since Jesus Christ, nor for enquiry since the Evangelist," asking rhetorically, "What has Athens to do with Jerusalem, or the academy with the Church?"

These are the cases and quotations beloved of atheist apologists, taken to demonstrate beyond all reasonable doubt Christianity's backward, obscurantist, anti-scientific, "faith"-obsessed retardations. The reality, of course, is much more complex than such caricatures suggest. As Peter Harrison shows in his book *The Territories of Science and Religion*, to claim that science and religion were at war in the first millennium—or even much of the second—would be like claiming that Israel and Egypt were at war in 1600; the entities, such as we understand them, simply did not exist then.

Thus the Church Fathers rejected not science—as we would certainly anachronistically call it at that time—but those philosophies that drew false conclusions from "scientific" activities. They, like everyone else in their culture, understood *scientia* as a path to *sapientia* or wisdom. Their reservations were usually not with the practice of *scientia* but with the conclusions some philosophers drew from studying the natural world (and in this they were not alone: Cicero once remarked that there was nothing so absurd that some philosopher had not already said it). As a rule, the Fathers refused the idea that the natural world was itself divine (ironically an important move toward a kind of naturalism, and one that is insufficiently recognized by modern apologists), and often assimilated natural philosophical ideas rather than rejected them wholesale.

If there is rather less in these various examples, stretching back from Swift to Tertullian, of scientific obscurantism than atheist apologists assume, they nonetheless constitute an important series of counterexamples for those who wish to show that science sprang naturally from the womb of Christianity, in a labor of almost beatific tranquility.

4

The manner of Christianity's midwifery might, then, have been complex but it is undeniable nonetheless. Although various possible accounts vie with one another here—an intellectual shift of this magnitude is hardly amenable to single explanations, and is hardly, therefore, an uncontested subject among modern historians—one undoubtedly key aspect lies in how nature came to be seen in the early modern period. Several things happened here to effect a change.

One was the European discovery of the New World. Not only did this demonstrate beyond all doubt that the ancients had not known everything there was to know but it produced, over the course of the sixteenth century, details of new-found flora and fauna that didn't fit into classical natural-historical classification. Not only was new knowledge possible, but it was necessary; the old way of reading the world failed to explain it.

This was happening at the same time as a new, or at least a fresh, way of reading texts was gaining ground. The later middle ages witnessed a trend toward the vernacular in a wide range of texts, and with this growing interest in translation there was a simultaneous move from "inspirational" to "philological" understandings of texts. The understanding of words came to be grounded "horizontally," by grasping their philological context, rather than vertically, by rooting their understanding in some divine and inspired authorship or, in the case of the Vulgate translation of the Bible, translation.

This certainly applied to legal texts. This was the period in which Lorenzo Valla finally disproved the authenticity of the Donation of Constantine, the document that purportedly witnessed the emperor Constantine's donation of authority over the Western empire to the pope but was in fact an eighth-century forgery. And it also applied to sacred texts. The medieval period had developed a complex fourfold system of scriptural reading. Everything, from the insignificant pelican of Psalm 102 (now more often translated desert owl) to the city of Jerusalem itself could, in theory, be read in a number of symbolic ways: the literal, the moral (how you should act), the allegorical (what you should believe), and the anagogical (what you should hope for). What was really important about the pelican or about Jerusalem was to be found primarily in what it symbolized, not in the fact it was a bird or a city.

What went for God's book of words could also be applied to his book of works. In Gaukroger's words, "the understanding of the physical world fostered in the Church Fathers was one in which an explanation of physical phenomena took the form of what those phenomena signified." It was an approach to nature that long outlasted the Fathers and came to form the basis of medieval natural philosophy. "This whole sensible world," wrote Hugh of St. Victor in the twelfth century, "is like a kind of book written by the finger of God . . . and each particular creature is somewhat like a figure . . . instituted by the divine will to manifest the invisible things of God's wisdom." Nature, like Scripture, was to be understood primarily symbolically.

The fourfold reading of Scripture was, of course, aggressively challenged and rejected by the Reformers, who cleaned away multiple readings of the Scriptures like so many barnacles from a boat. *Sola scriptura*—Scripture alone—was the rallying cry, and a literal reading alone was the cry at the heart of that. And, according to Peter Harrison, where scriptural interpretation led, so the interpretation of nature followed. Just as the words of God—and indeed words generally—came to be best understood by their relation to other words, rather than, say, to the things in heaven that they somehow symbolized, so the works of God were to be understood by their relationship with one another rather than what they might have symbolized. Henceforth, pelicans were to be understood as pelicans, cities as cities, nature as nature. Nature's intelligibility now came from its taxonomic order, how it related to other bits of nature, rather than from its symbolic power.

Understanding nature on its own terms rather than according to any divine symbolism, however, did not mean abandoning ideas that nature had symbolic potential. Put another way, this new way of "reading" nature did not mean admitting that it had nothing to say about God.

In the first instance, natural philosophers argued, with good scriptural justification, that studying God's works did him honor. As Francis Bacon put it in *The Advancement of Learning*:

> For as the Psalms and other Scriptures do often invite us to consider and magnify the great and wonderful works of God, so if we should rest only in the contemplation of the exterior of them as they first offer themselves to our senses, we should do a like injury unto the majesty of God.

Or, as Calvin remarked in his commentary on Genesis, the study of astronomy is not to be reprobated for not only is astronomy "very pleasant" but also useful, for "it cannot be denied that this art unfolds the admirable wisdom of God."

Moreover, as Peter Harrison explains in his book *The Fall of Man and the Foundations of Science*, many saw in the activity of natural philosophy one of the means by which the loss of Adam's fall might be made good. Studying nature could help recover lost Adamic knowledge and controlling it could help restore Adam's lost dominion. Again, in Francis Bacon's words:

> For man by the fall fell at the same time from his state of innocence and from his dominion over creation. Both of these losses however can even in this life be in some part repaired; the former by religion and faith, the latter by arts and sciences.

Or, in the even more forceful words of Thomas Sprat, making his case for the early Royal Society:

> This was the first service, that Adam perform'd to his Creator, when he obey'd him in mustring, and naming, and looking into the Nature of all the Creatures. This had bin the only religion, if men had continued innocent in Paradise, and had not wanted a redemption.

The Fellows of the Royal Society were doing nothing less than forging a new Eden.

Indeed, this concept of the Fall went further still in its effect on the development of the experiment, the thing that was so self-evidently absurd to Gulliver. The Fall affected man's intellectual abilities as much as his moral ones, and he could no longer rely on thinking his way to the truth. Instead, he had to feel his way there, step by hesitant, faltering step. Contrary to the popular view of Enlightenment rationalism powering its way toward scientific success by having raised its eyes to the glories of the human intellect, Harrison suggests that

> the birth of modern experimental science was not attended with a new awareness of the powers and capacities of human reason, but rather the opposite—a consciousness of the manifold deficiencies of the intellect, of the misery of the human condition, and of the limited scope of scientific achievement.

This, Harrison acknowledges, is an incomplete story, and the impact of such a fallen anthropology was stronger in those places (like England) that were more affected by Calvinism than it was in those like Northern Italy that saw comparable scientific achievements in the early seventeenth century. Moreover, it is a story that is undermined, or at least qualified, by the equally powerful motivator that the universe, made by a rational God, was therefore intelligible to his rational creatures. Nature was characterized by an order that was

105

comprehensible to humans precisely because they were made in the image of its creator. The mind of God gave order to nature and as human minds reflected that mind, albeit imperfectly, they were in a unique position to detect nature's order. God and humans could, in effect, converse in the language of mathematics.

If to all this we might add the transformed understanding of vocation in the Reformation period, which further underlined how the natural philosopher might bring glory to God in his works, it becomes easy to see how the first tentative seeds of the natural philosophers might grow and a culture of science might take root in this amenable soil. In Gaukroger's words, by such an intellectual shift, or series of shifts, "the natural philosopher has become not only religiously motivated bur religiously empowered."

5

In all this, therefore, Christianity served as science's apt and able midwife. There was, however, a large and significant accident that further served to strengthen this role.

All the intellectual movements outlined above were taking place on the side of a volcano, which erupted with more or less frequency and violence throughout the sixteenth and first half of the seventeenth centuries. Science took root as it did in the midst of an epistemological crisis of unprecedented magnitude for Europe. The theo-political battles of the sixteenth and seventeenth centuries saw confessional blocks do everything in their power to undermine each other's foundations. And the Bible, the fount of all true and reliable knowledge, was invariably caught in the crossfire of this theological battle, and was damaged in the process.

The discipline of biblical study predated the Reformation. The year before Luther had pinned his theses to Wittenberg's church door, the greatest European humanist, Desiderius Erasmus, published his *Novum instrumentum* or New Instrument, which printed the New Testament in its original Greek, alongside a new Latin translation, and made about 400 changes to the traditional Vulgate translation (following it up with over 300 pages of notes explaining them).

Humanist textual criticism was not a problem for Catholics, who understood Scripture as having been born and formed within the

Church's magisterium and who were thus open to it being studied accordingly. Nor was it necessarily a problem for Reformers, many of whom had been trained as humanist scholars and whose call "To the sources" entailed the recognition that Scripture, being the Word of God, needed to be understood as accurately as possible. It was, after all, a Protestant biblical scholar, Louis Cappel, who compiled a list of thousands of textual variants in the Hebrew and Greek biblical texts. However, when different factions began to question each others' basis for biblical interpretation, they also questioned the texts on which their interpretation was founded, and biblical criticism as an anti-Christian discipline was born.

Protestants claimed that Jerome's Vulgate was error-strewn. Catholics responded that the original Hebrew text, which St. Jerome had drawn on for his translation, and which was now lost, had been superior to the current Hebrew text, which had been corrupted over the centuries. Catholics sought to undermine the Hebrew Masoretic text, which Protestants judged authoritative for the Old Testament, by showing that it was the product of historical process and human interventions, a line further supported by study of the Samaritan Pentateuch, which was first obtained from the Levant in the early seventeenth century. The question of textual reliability, compositional process, and authorship thus became another weapon in the confessional battles of the time.

Both parties found ways to accommodate the new learning (although the doubts that loomed over the biblical text hit Protestants harder than they did Catholics), but both were discomfited by the way scholarship appeared to pick at the unity of Scripture, casting doubts on its veracity, focusing on its mutability and fragility, and seeing its formation as a human process. Moreover, when textual arguments were deployed by one Christian faction against another, they became weapons of mass destruction (not least as they were later picked up and deployed by more comprehensive skeptics against Christianity as a whole).

It was into this breach that natural philosophy rode. Already dignified and empowered by theology, natural philosophy came to its rescue—or so it seemed at the time—by proving those things that Scripture and exegesis could not. As early as the 1530s, the German reformer Philip Melanchthon made natural philosophy the central part of his defence of Lutheranism, his early work repeatedly drawing attention to the skill of God in creating different parts of the body for different purposes and claiming that anatomy is the beginning of theology.

Later theologians were still more explicit about its apologetic potential. The French philosopher Jean Bodin explained

> how valuable is it that those who cannot be dragged by any precepts of divine law or oracles of the prophets from their ingrained folly or led to the worship of the true deity, are forced by the most certain demonstrations of this science, as if under the application of torture and questioning, to reject all impiety and to adore one and the same eternal deity.

For Bacon, such studies "minister a singular help and preservative against unbelief and error." So it was that theologians began to pile their eggs into scientific baskets and a culture of science became not only possible, admirable, commendable, and respectable, but also increasingly obligatory and ubiquitous.

6

It would not be true to say that the rest is history. Indeed, to end the story at the end of the seventeenth century is to omit some of the aesthetic, social, political, and philosophical quagmires that have threatened time and again to engulf the practices and objectives of science. Romantic sensibilities, brutal social Darwinian extrapolations, political orthodoxies such as that which underpinned Lysenkoism, and extreme postmodernities that denied all truth by their own: all of these have, at times, threatened—and indeed on occasion succeeded—to turn people against science and reverse and unmake the West's scientific culture.

Each of these, except perhaps the third, shows some signs of life today, but it is clearly the last that most vexes our more prominent scientific apologists, at least if some of the essays in Richard Dawkins's *A Devil's Chaplain* is anything to go by. The problem with this, however, is that such threats, however real they are, are liable to provoke a disproportionate response among scientific apologists and encourage science's own totalizing tendencies, "the gradual assimilation of all cognitive values to scientific ones," as Gaukroger puts it.

This is not a new temptation. Writing of the views of the mid-eighteenth-century French atheist *philosophe* Claude Adrien Helvétius, Isaiah Berlin explained that, by Helvétius's logic:

> scientists know the truth, therefore scientists are virtuous, therefore scientists make us happy . . . What we need is a universe governed by scientists, because to be a good man, to be a wise man, to be a scientist, to be a virtuous man are, in the end, the same thing.

It was this that led Berlin to label Helvétius as one of his six "enemies of human liberty" in his 1952 lectures on the subject.

Less than a century after Helvétius, such totalizing views received their most earnest and thorough systemization in the eccentric thought of Auguste Comte and his Positivists, and such views have hovered on the periphery of serious thought ever since. Threats to a scientific culture mean that these peripheral views sometimes move closer to the center. Recent alarms about creationism and postmodernity, coupled with the vague mixture of confusion, disinterest, and contempt that is shown toward science in an age of C. P. Snow's "two cultures," means that there has been much activity here of late, with books aplenty showing how science—evolution being the current discipline of choice—serves as a firm and secure basis for morality, politics, philosophy, society, and, of course, religion and much else besides. The child that Christianity helped deliver threatens to destroy it.

I doubt it will. After all, it has been threatening to do so since at least Helvétius's time but, as historians like Harrison, Gaukroger, and John Hedley Brooke have convincingly shown, for all those voices claiming that "science" is at war with and utterly disproves "religion," there have been plenty more claiming that the relationship between the two is much more complex and, indeed, more amenable than that. Moreover, it seems that when societies lose their religious faith it is rarely because of "science."

Nonetheless, the stand-off continues, sometimes aggressively, sometimes comically. "Science is omnipotent," the Oxford chemist Peter Atkins once told the Christian philosopher William Lane Craig in a debate. Craig demurred. "Do you deny that science cannot (*sic*) account for everything?" Atkins hit back. Craig did. Atkins pressed him. "So what can't it account for?"

A good number of things, Craig replied, before going on to list five to an increasingly ashen-faced Atkins. There are:

> logical and mathematical proofs . . . science presupposes logic and maths . . . to try to prove them by science would be arguing in a circle . . . [there are] metaphysical truths like other minds, or that the external world is real, or that the past was not created five minutes ago with the appearance of age . . . [there are] ethical beliefs about statements of value . . . [there are] aesthetic judgments . . . the beautiful like the good cannot be scientifically proven . . . [and] most remarkably, science itself; science cannot be justified by the scientific method, science is permeated with unprovable assumptions.

Just very occasionally, scientists today can appear as silly as those Lemuel Gulliver met at the Grand Academy of Lagado.

8

"No Doubts as to How One Ought to Act": Darwin's Doubts and His Faith

———•·•———

1

In the year before Charles Darwin married Emma Wedgwood, the two cousins discussed religion. In a short chapter entitled "Religious Belief" in his autobiography, written many years later and intended only for immediate circulation, Darwin located his loss of Christian faith within precisely this period, "from my return to England [from the *Beagle* on] Oct. 2, 1836 to my marriage Jan. 29, 1839." In it he highlighted three concerns in particular that caused him to lose his religion.

Darwin had growing doubts about the reliability of Scripture, both Old Testament and New ("the Gospels cannot be proved to have been written simultaneously with the events . . . [and] they differ in many important details, far too important . . . to be admitted as the usual inaccuracies of eye-witnesses"). He had moral qualms with some of the teachings and stories of the Old Testament (the Old Testament "attribute[d] to God the feelings of a revengeful tyrant . . . [and] was no more to be trusted than the sacred books of the Hindoos, or the beliefs of any barbarian"), and skepticism concerning the philosophical coherence and scientific credibility of the biblical world view ("The more we know of the fixed laws of nature the more incredible do miracles become").

Darwin's account of his loss of faith is overly schematized. Indeed, his biographer, Janet Browne, describes the entire autobiography as "just as much an exercise in camouflage—a disguise—as it was a methodical laying out of the bare bones of his existence." Nevertheless, there is little doubt that, by 1839, Darwin came to realize that his heretofore "orthodox" Christian faith was nothing like the case.

And this was a problem for Emma. Emma Wedgwood was an intelligent, sincere, and devout believer. Religion had been a point of tension between her family and his, ever since his grandfather, Erasmus, had mocked Emma's, Josiah, for his Unitarianism, which Erasmus had called "a featherbed to catch a falling Christian." Darwin's own father knew something of his son's growing skepticism, which he probably shared, and had advised caution, but Charles was nothing if not an honest man, and confided his doubts to Emma on a visit to her in July 1838.

There is no record of what Darwin actually said to her or what her immediate reaction was, but it clearly caused some difficulties and occasioned a series of letters and notes from Emma to Charles. These offer an important and often moving counterpart to Darwin's own much later and resolutely factual account, with Emma, in her gentle and tentative way, encouraging her fiancé to open himself up to the evidence for and, more importantly, an experience of the Christian faith.

The last of the letters dates from a few weeks *after* their marriage and constitutes Emma's fullest note on the subject. Unable to "say exactly what I wish to say," she put her thoughts on paper. In doing so, she revealed a telling detail from one of their early marital conversations on the topic. "I do not quite agree with you in what you once said," she wrote, "that luckily there were no doubts as to how one ought to act." On the contrary, "I think prayer is an instance to the contrary, in one case it is a positive duty & perhaps not in the other." She continued in a conciliatory matter, "but I dare say you meant in actions which concern others & then I agree with you almost if not quite."

This is an enlightening aside, revealing how the young Darwin, and even the devout Emma, like so many people in early Victorian Britain, was unable to imagine that Christianity made any particular or unique ethical or behavioral demands. This was not the criticism levelled by some Chartists at the time, namely that the teachings of Christ made no difference to the lives of his so-called followers, sated as they were on the fruits of establishment and social security. Rather, Darwin's point was that the contours of a good life were evident to any educated, morally sensitive gentleman; it made precious little difference as to whether or not one held to the creeds of Christianity: there could be no serious doubts about how one ought to act.

In this Darwin revealed himself as blissfully unaware of the extent to which Christianity had shaped the cultural waters in which he comfortably swam. Unlike the majority of his countrymen, this was certainly not because he was unaware of other cultures and ethical standards. His time on the *Beagle* had been shared, at first, with three Fuegians, returning to the southernmost tip of South America as missionaries, and he vividly recalls his first, shocking encounter with the "wild and savage" natives of the Tierra del Fuego in his *Voyage of the Beagle*. Thirty years later he wrote in *The Descent of Man*, "There is no evidence that man was aboriginally endowed with the ennobling belief in the existence of an Omnipotent God." Darwin knew how very different—religiously and ethically—other cultures could be.

Such sensitivity to the true breadth of religious, ethical, and cultural conditions seems not to have disabused him of the notion that "there were no doubts as to how one ought to act," however. In that regard, Darwin gives us a window on how it is that inattentiveness to the deep foundations of our own culture can desensitize us to the fragility of the social and ethical edifices we build on them.

2

Darwin did not claim to be a serious religious thinker. Indeed, he repeatedly insisted that such issues were beyond his capabilities and that they left him terribly muddled.

He wrote very little on the subject. Mankind is famously absent from *The Origin of Species*, and Darwin's only book to engage with Christianity in any detail, if you exclude his posthumously published *Autobiography*, is *The Voyage of the Beagle*, in which he writes at some length and wholly positively about the work of missionaries in the South Pacific.

The reasons for this reticence are complex. Darwin did not want to upset Emma. He did not want to upset public opinion in any way that might retard the reception of his theory. And he generally approved of the religious influence on society. Most significantly, Darwin was a scientist, not a theologian or philosopher, and his interest in both these disciplines was frankly minimal. He was often attacked by theologians and he was often attacked ignorantly by them. Edward Pusey, Regius Professor of Hebrew at Oxford and a leading member of the

Oxford Movement, disliked the idea of evolution and accused Darwin in a sermon of forming his theory in order to attack Christianity. Yet as Darwin himself insisted in a letter to the botanist Nicholas Ridley, "Pusey was mistaken in imagining that I wrote *the Origin* [*of Species*] with any relation whatever to Theology." In spite of what critics thought then (and indeed today), Darwin was not interested enough in religion to attack it, whether openly or under the cloak of natural selection.

Like most people of his age and class, he was brought up a Christian, albeit one who came from unusually skeptical stock. He attended the local Unitarian chapel in Shrewsbury until his mother died, when he was eight. He then moved to the parish church and thereafter to boarding school and to the study of medicine at Edinburgh.

Few letters survive from his Edinburgh days but those that do reveal, at best, a lukewarm religiosity. "Dear Charles," his sister Caroline wrote to him in 1826, "I hope you read the bible & not only because you think it wrong not to read it, but with the wish of learning there what is necessary to feel & do to go to heaven after you die." A few days later she wrote again in a similar vein, confiding that "I often regret myself that when I was younger & fuller of pursuits & high spirits I was not more religious—but it is very difficult to be so habitually."

Darwin's father was vexed not by his son's lack of Bible reading but by his lack of medical ambition, and insisted he find useful employment. If medicine didn't suit him, then it had to be the Church. Early-nineteenth-century Anglicanism was nothing like as broad a church as it was to become, but it would nonetheless be an exaggeration to say that one needed a burning commitment to the gospel to be ordained. It is telling that when, a few years later, Darwin's uncle, Josiah, tried to persuade his father to allow Darwin to travel on the *Beagle*, he reasoned that not only would such a journey not be "in any degree disreputable to his character as a Clergyman," but that "the pursuit of Natural History" was in fact "very suitable to a clergyman." A serious personal belief in God was no bar to the Anglican ministry, but nor was it a necessity.

To his credit, Darwin paused. In his autobiography he recorded how "I asked for some time to consider [my father's offer]." There was much that appealed in the life of a country clergyman but Darwin knew that his personal convictions were weak. "From what little I had heard and thought on the subject," he relates in his autobiography, "I had scruples about declaring my belief in all the dogmas of the Church of England." His hesitation is testimony to his integrity. How he dealt with it is testimony to the nature of the Christianity he was expected to profess.

Darwin read some books. Specifically, he read Bishop John Pearson's *Exposition of the Creed*, and "a few other books on divinity," including *The Evidence of Christianity derived from its Nature and Reception* by the Revd John Bird Sumner, published in 1821. Pearson's book had proved popular and influential when first published, but since that was 1659, it was a little out of date by the time Darwin got to it. Darwin was nonetheless impressed. "I did not then in the least doubt the strict and literal truth of every word in the Bible [and] soon persuaded myself that our Creed must be fully accepted." Duly persuaded and deeming himself "orthodox," he agreed to ordination.

There is no reason to doubt the reality of Darwin's "orthodoxy" at the time, but it is important to note what *kind* of orthodoxy it was. "Orthodox" for Darwin meant being able to assent to basic Christian doctrines. It was logical, objective, rationalistic, and demonstrable. Christianity was, first and foremost, a proof to be established.

Cambridge did little to change that. Indeed, it rather encouraged it. Most importantly, it immersed him in the most influential theologian of the day, William Paley. Paley's *Principles of Moral and Political Philosophy* and his *Evidences of Christianity* were compulsory reading at Cambridge, but it was his (optional) *Natural Theology* that most impressed Darwin. *Natural Theology* transferred the arguments from physical design, which had proved so popular in the seventeenth and eighteenth centuries, into arguments from biological design. Nature, Paley argued, contains "every manifestation of design." His book examined a vast range of these "manifestations," and concluded triumphantly that "design must have had a designer . . . That designer must have been a person [and] that person is God." Darwin was impressed and Paleyian natural theology thereby became a cornerstone of his faith.

3

That faith was lost in the years on and after the *Beagle*. His years on the *Beagle* did not destroy Darwin's ordered, propositional, Paleyian Christianity but they did disturb its foundations.

Sailing round the tip of South America, he encountered people on the Tierra del Fuego who were shockingly barbarous, even animalistic. Perhaps the line between humans and other species was thinner and more permeable than comfortable Anglican archdeacons imagined? Travelling further up the west coast, he experienced an earthquake and volcanic eruption, which shocked him. "A bad earthquake at once destroys the oldest associations," he wrote in *The Voyage of the Beagle*.

> The world, the very emblem of all that is solid, has moved beneath our feet like a crust over a fluid;—one second of time has conveyed to the mind a strange idea of insecurity, which hours of reflection would never have created.

All this seemed to suggest that the real earth was indifferent, rather than tailored to human needs as the natural theologians of the eighteenth century imagined.

Such observations perturbed his Christian foundations, but it was only the years after his return in 1836 that saw the building constructed on these foundations totter and fall. Darwin was a meticulous, almost obsessive note taker, and a series of notebooks from this period trace the development of his theory and, interestingly, the ways in which he worked to accommodate it with belief in God.

First, there was the problem of special creation. Evolution wrecked the idea that God had made each species separately. But then, was that such a great idea? Was it not "grander" to see all life emerging through a continuous process of law-governed evolution? How much more appealing was evolution than the idea "that since the time of the Silurian [God] has made a long succession of vile molluscous animals"? Special creation was nothing to boast about. "How beneath the dignity of him, who is supposed to have said let there be light & there was light."

Second, there was the idea that humans may not, in fact, be that different from other species. "Man—wonderful man . . . with divine face turned towards heaven . . . he is not a deity, his end under present form will come . . . he is no exception," he wrote in Notebook C, sounding a bit like an Old Testament prophet.

This upset human pride, but there was more. What if key human attributes like thought, morality, and religiosity were not distinctively "spiritual" qualities but rather material outworkings of the evolutionary process? Coming from a world view in which the material and the spiritual were necessarily distinct and opposed, this was a significant challenge. Where did it leave personal morality? Where did it leave human conscience? Where did it leave the Last Judgement?

Finally, there was the problem of suffering. This was not a new problem, as Darwin acknowledged, but his theory made it newly significant. Evolution replaced William Paley's "happy world . . . [of] delighted existence" with the pitiless one of Thomas Malthus, in which a "dreadful but quiet war of organic beings [was] going on in the peaceful woods & smiling fields."

Suffering, for Darwin, was a serious intellectual problem, but it was to become a serious personal one too. His eldest daughter, Annie, had long suffered from ill health, which Darwin feared she had inherited from him, and in 1851 he took her to Malvern for treatment before returning to Emma who was eight months pregnant. Two weeks later he received an urgent message. Annie had contracted a fever. Darwin returned instantly, to be faced with a changed child. "You would not in the least recognize her," he told Emma, "with her poor hard, sharp pinched features; I could only bear to look at her by forgetting our former dear Annie."

The following week was the worst of his life. Annie rallied, then sank. She showed signs of recovery and then of fading fast. Unable to eat, she slowly wasted away. The doctors remained quietly confident. Darwin sat, holding her hand, alternately overjoyed and distraught. Eventually, she died, aged ten. Most Victorian families lost children—Darwin himself lost two others in infancy—but Annie was his favorite and he had witnessed every last, degrading moment of her short life. The experience nearly destroyed him. It certainly destroyed what was left of his faith. He wrote a short, painfully moving account of her life, and then never spoke about her again.

His *theory* of evolution had alerted him to the reality and apparent ubiquity of suffering but he could—or, at least, could try to—rationalize and cope with that. "From death, famine, rapine, and the concealed war of nature we can see that *the highest good, which we can conceive*, the creation of the higher animals has directly come," he wrote at the end of his 1842 sketch for what would become *The Origin of Species*. The key question was, did that "highest good" justify "the concealed war of nature"? Darwin's tentative theoretical answer, at least in 1842, was "yes." But with Annie's death, suffering moved from being a theory to being horribly, painfully real. Whatever faith he had in the loving, just God of Christianity, it died with his daughter in Malvern.

4

Darwin thereby became an atheist with regard to the Christian God. He was never, however, an atheist in the full sense of the word. He remained a "theist" throughout the 1850s and '60s, although the God he believed in was now the God of first causes and, properly speaking, he was more deist than theist during this period.

In the final decades of his life he was, in essence, pulled in two directions. In one regard, as he wrote to his cousin Frances Wedgwood in 1861, "the mind refuses to look at this universe, being what it is, without having been designed." This was a recurring theme. "One cannot look at this Universe with all living productions & man without believing that all has been intelligently designed," he told John Herschel, the grand old man of science, at about the same time.

And yet, he continued, "when I look to each individual organism, I can see no evidence of this [design]." "Where one would most expect design," he told Wedgwood, "viz. in the structure of a sentient being, the more I think on the subject, the less I can see proof of design." "I am driven to two opposite conclusions," he admitted to Henry Acland. "My theology is a simple muddle," he told Joseph Hooker. "I cannot look at the Universe as the result of blind chance, yet I can see no evidence of beneficent Design."

The "muddle" was well expressed in one of the last letters he wrote, to the philosopher William Graham. Darwin had recently read Graham's book *Creed of Science* and, unusually for him, was writing cold to thank him for it. "It is a very long time since any other book has interested me so much," he said. "You have expressed my inward conviction, though far more vividly and clearly than I could have done," he praised Graham, "that the Universe is not the result of chance." Much as he liked the book, however, he did not agree with everything Graham had to say:

> There are some points in your book which I cannot digest. The chief one is that the existence of so-called natural laws implies purpose. I cannot see this ... [assuming] the laws as we now know them ... the law of gravitation ... of the conservation of energy, of the atomic theory, &c. &c. hold good, ... I cannot see that there is then necessarily any purpose [to them].

Darwin's agnosticism went deeper even than this tension implies, however. Indeed, he was not simply agnostic in the sense of not knowing whether or not there was a God, but he came to doubt whether the human mind, being evolved from that of a "lower" animal, could know such things. His autobiography explains how he was impressed by "the extreme difficulty or rather impossibility of conceiving this immense and wonderful universe, including man with his capacity of looking far backwards and far into futurity, as the result of blind chance or necessity." This was the argument from cosmic as opposed to biological design that sustained his fluctuating theism for the last twenty years. "When thus reflecting I feel compelled to look to a First Cause having an intelligent mind in some degree analogous to that of man; and I deserve to be called a Theist." But then came what we might call "the monkey puzzle." "Can the mind of man, which has, as I fully believe, been developed from a mind as low as that possessed by the lowest animal, be trusted when it draws such grand conclusions?" Darwin asked rhetorically. "May not these be the result of the connection between cause and effect which strikes us as a necessary one, but probably depends merely on inherited experience?" Not only did Darwin now not know about God. He didn't know whether he *could* know.

5

On September 5, 1834, Darwin was travelling through Chile, a few miles south of Santiago. In the evening he and his companions reached a comfortable farmhouse "where there were several very pretty señoritas." Throughout his travels Darwin had often stopped off to "admire the brilliancy of the decorations" of the gloriously baroque Catholic churches of the Continent. "It is impossible not to respect the fervor which appears to reign during the Catholic service as compared with the Protestant," he remarked in his diary. He mentioned his aesthetically motivated churchgoing to his pretty señoritas and was taken aback by their shock.

> They were much horrified at my having entered one of their churches out of mere curiosity [and] asked me, "Why do you not become a Christian—for our religion is certain?" I assured them I was a sort of Christian.

Darwin meant, of course, an Anglican *sort* of Christian rather than a Roman Catholic one. But the phrase "a sort of Christian" has connotations beyond its intended usage. In many ways it serves as an apt if accidental description of the whole Christian faith he lost.

That Christian faith was genuine. Any attempt to show that Darwin wasn't *really* a Christian before or during his *Beagle* days would be an exercise in sophistry. Darwin was a confirmed Christian and an Anglican one at that. He immersed himself in the writings of Anglican theologians and assented to the creeds and the Thirty-Nine Articles, although he later wrote that "It never struck me how illogical it was to say that I believed in what I could not understand and what is in fact unintelligible."

That recognized, Darwin was a particular *sort* of Christian, a sort typical of his time and class. Darwin's Christian faith, up to and including his *Beagle* days, was orthodox, but orthodox in a particular, early-nineteenth-century, socially secure, Anglican kind of way. Pearson and Sumner offer a good indication of the neat, rational, orthodox Christianity to which Darwin adhered in his pre-*Beagle* days. Not so much a personal commitment to the person and work of Christ, still less an affecting encounter with the Holy Spirit, this Christianity was a series of propositions to be accepted, a hypothesis to be satisfactorily established, an argument to be won.

Reason, particularly reason based on the natural world, was paramount. Darwin's was a Christian faith based more on rational defences of the logic and coherence of the Apostles' Creed or the

Thirty-Nine Articles than it was a personal commitment to or moving experience of Jesus Christ. There was little space for John Wesley's "heart strangely warmed."

In this he was simply an inheritor of over one hundred years of theological tradition, in which the shift to natural philosophy that had occurred in the mid-seventeenth century gradually began to edge aside the more distinctively Christian justifications for Christian faith.

Such a view was hardly ubiquitous, even among leading Christians. Some years before *Natural Theology* was published, John Wesley, following St. Paul, had observed in a sermon on "The General Deliverance":

> How true then is that word, "God saw everything that he had made: and behold it was very good!" But how far is this from being the present case! In what a condition is the whole lower world!—to say nothing of inanimate nature, wherein all the elements seem to be out of course, and by turns to fight against man. Since man rebelled against his Maker, in what a state is all animated nature! Well might the Apostle say of this: "The whole creation groaneth and travaileth together in pain until now." This directly refers to the brute creation in what state this is at present we are now to consider.

In a similar vein, a few years later John Henry Newman, by then the most famous Roman Catholic in the country, remarked of Paley's *Natural Theology* in his 1852 lectures on *The Idea of a University*:

> It has been taken out of its place, has been put too prominently forward, and thereby has almost been used as an instrument against Christianity ... Physical [i.e., Natural] theology cannot ... tell us one word about Christianity proper; it cannot be Christian, in any true sense, at all ... [indeed] I do not hesitate to say that ... this so-called science tends, if it occupies the mind, to dispose it against Christianity.

But Darwin had not grown up with or into either Wesley's or Newman's forms of British Christianity. Darwin's was true primarily because the natural world pointed to structure, harmony, and happiness. It was no surprise, therefore, that when he first recognized that the natural world was not as ordered, purposive or benign as had been thought, the Christian structure that towered about these foundations toppled.

121

6

But not, crucially, the ethical structure that he had constructed with it. True to his early exchanges with Emma, the couple shared a wonderfully happy, intimate, robust, secure marriage, a true meeting of souls if not necessarily minds. For all Emma's Christian devotion and Charles's agnostic doubts, they did not disagree on how one ought to act, even when it came to the role of Christianity in public life. It appeared as if beliefs didn't make a difference to ethics, at least as far as the Darwins were concerned.

Darwin had long been a supporter of missionary activity, despite the fact that the *Beagle's* original Fuegian mission had proved a catastrophe.* Such a disaster notwithstanding, Darwin's time on the *Beagle* had imbued him with an appreciation of missionary activity that did not dim with age. He was delighted to learn, later in life, that a successful mission had been established in Tierra del Fuego, and he subsequently accepted an invitation to be an honorary member of the South American Missionary Society, to which he made small donations.

Closer to home, Darwin served as the treasurer of the Coal and Clothing Club, which helped provide for the needy in Downe village, where he and Emma moved in 1842. He proposed an investment scheme that would raise funds for the village poor, and when it was set up as the Downe Friendly Society he administered its funds. He was a member of the parish council and regularly contributed to the village Sunday School. He oversaw a former schoolroom in the parish, in which his family set up a temperance reading room. When James Fegan, a local evangelist, requested use of the room in 1880 to bring his tent revival meetings indoors, Darwin not only granted permission but told him, "your services have done more for the village

---

* When the *Beagle* returned after a month to the settlement in which their missionary, Richard Matthews, had been put ashore, the crew found him in a state of nervous collapse. According to Darwin's diary, "from the moment of our leaving, a regular system of plunder commenced." Matthews had lost nearly everything. He was continually hassled by Fuegians, who surrounded his house "night & day." Thinking they were after more of his provisions, Matthews "met them with presents." But it wasn't enough. The Fuegians indicated that they wanted to "strip him & pluck all the hairs out of his face & body." "I think we returned just in time to save his life," Darwin observed.

in a few months than all our efforts for many years . . . Through your services I do not know that there is a drunkard left in the village." Darwin may no longer have been a Christian but he happily lived the life of the country squire, with all the Christian charitable activity and support that involved.

And yet in his later years it slowly became clear that the idea that faith and morals were independent of one another was not so easy to sustain, and the irony is that it was his work on evolution that helped prize the two apart.

Darwin's work appeared to show that Thomas Malthus's—or indeed Thomas Hobbes's—vision of the universal war of all against all was simply the way of things. Competition was the law of nature and, as such, should be the law of mankind. It was through the processes of natural selection that the weak and frail were weeded out, the strong provided with the resources they needed to flourish, and the greater good achieved. Such, of course, was the message that many, most notably Herbert Spencer, who coined the phrase "the survival of the fittest," took from Darwin's work. Darwin corresponded with Spencer, telling him in 1860 that "of my numerous (Private) critics, you are almost the only one who has put the philosophy of the argument, as it seems to me, in a fair way." But he also recoiled from the harsh implications of Spencer's Social Darwinism, in spite of recognizing his ideas in its foundations. Spencer's social outworking of Darwin's theory showed that there were other, very different ways of living in the world; ways that had, in Darwin's mind, a better claim to reflect *reality* than Christianity did, but ways that did not fit with the ethical and behavioral presuppositions that he—and Emma—judged so self-evident. Darwinism mandated Social Darwinism, according to Spencer and others. Darwin disagreed, but without any philosophically robust reasons for doing so.

This tension was demonstrated in an exchange Darwin had with Charles Bradlaugh in 1877. Bradlaugh was Victorian England's greatest public atheist and no stranger to controversy. Along with Annie Besant, a prominent radical, socialist, orator, and women's rights activist, he was on trial for publishing *Fruits of Philosophy: Or the Private Companion of Young Married People* by Charles Knowlton, an American writer and atheist, for which he and Besant had penned a preface. *Fruits of Philosophy* advocated various means of birth control as a way of avoiding what many feared was the impending Malthusian crisis, in which population growth outstripped production, and mankind was faced with a future of epidemic, war, plague, and famine. Abstinence, Malthus's preferred solution, was, according to Knowlton, Besant, and Bradlaugh, utterly inadequate and unrealistic. Only birth control could stave off disaster.

The book's previous publisher had been prosecuted for obscenity but Besant and Bradlaugh were undeterred. Moreover, Darwinism, now established as a science, showed Malthus's theories to be true and Darwin, increasingly one of the country's most respected figures, had drawn explicitly and crucially on Malthus. His voice might make all the difference to the trial, and so Bradlaugh wrote to him asking if he would testify on their behalf.

Darwin's response was telling. He replied to Bradlaugh on June 6, 1877, saying that he would prefer not to be a witness in court. This wasn't simply on account of Darwin's notoriously weak stomach and aversion to public prominence. He went on to say that he was strongly opposed to Bradlaugh and Besant's view. Although he had read only notices of their book, he told Bradlaugh that he believed artificial checks on the natural rate of human increase were very undesirable, and that the use of artificial means to prevent conception would destroy chastity and, ultimately, the family. Although he had not been a Christian, even in name, for nearly thirty years, Darwin appeared to hold resolutely to the personal and public morality that Christianity had bequeathed to Victorian Britain.

That morality was not, of course, to last, and it is curious to imagine what Darwin would have felt about the moral transition that Britain would undergo in the twentieth century. In the UK today, birth control is all but ubiquitous, and wholly uncontentious (indeed, ironically, it is only those few who still hold to Darwin's position who are judged in any way controversial in this now settled issue). More controversial is the number of underage girls taking birth control. According to one recent study, headed by Dr. Asia Rashed of the Institute of Pharmaceutical Science at King's College London, using GPs' data, around one in twenty underage girls—or about 75,000—in the UK are on the pill.

If this would have worried Darwin, one can only guess at what he would have thought about reported levels of promiscuity—according to one recent study, the average Briton today has had ten sexual partners (men having had twelve, women seven); or the number of abortions carried out each year—185,000 in 2013, with the under-18 abortion rate at 11.7 per 1,000 women, and the under-16 abortion rate at 2.6 per 1,000 women; or the level of divorce—249 a year when Darwin wrote to Charles Bradlaugh; 129,000 a year a century later (and around 120,000 today); or the fact that approximately a million children in Britain grow up today without a father in their lives.

The list could go on. The point is not to claim that the chastity and family values of mid-Victorian Britain were uniquely or incontrovertibly Christian. Most people today, including most Christians, recognize that they were unduly oppressive and severe. Rather it is to show that you don't need to go as far as the Social Darwinism erected on Darwin's and Malthus's understanding of reality, which was to have so harmful an impact in the twentieth century, to realize that moral convictions are not self-evident and that there were, in fact, plenty of doubts as to how one ought to act.

Darwin imagined that Christianity could fade from the heart and mind without any significant ethical or behavioral impact. He had faith that you could, in effect, maintain Christian ethics without maintaining Christianity. Yet shortly before he was born the great abolitionist William Wilberforce had written:

> The fatal habit of considering Christian morals as distinct from Christian doctrines insensibly gained strength. Thus the peculiar doctrines of Christianity went more and more out of sight and as might naturally have been expected, the moral system itself also began to wither and decay, being robbed of that which should have supplied it with life and nutriment.

The newly wed Darwin would have disagreed, yet one cannot but be left to wonder whether, by the end of his life, his encounters with Spencer, Bradlaugh, and Besant—alas he didn't live long enough to encounter Nietzsche—might have caused him to think otherwise.

9

The Religion of Christianity and the Religion of Human Rights

—————•‥•‥•—————

1

Shami Chakrabarti's book *On Liberty* ostensibly retells her "personal and political journey" as director of Liberty, the human rights organization. The organization was already of pensionable age when she joined on September 10, 2001, having begun in the crypt of St Martin-in-the-Fields in 1934, but Chakrabarti—and the events of the following day and their still-unfolding consequences—gave it a whole new lease of life. For all its biographic framing, however, this director's cut is, in effect, the story of human rights and, in particular, their recent history in Britain.

This has been somewhat turbulent, to put it mildly, rights being only just short of salvific for some and only just short of demonic for others. There is little doubt where Chakrabarti stands on this spectrum. Although she is not what she calls a human rights "fundamentalist"—she recognizes that very few rights are absolute and that the majority may be "interfered with" if done "proportionately [and] for . . . good reasons"—she nonetheless is unyielding in her belief that a full and principled adherence to legally enshrined human rights makes for a much better, fairer, and more secure society. If this sounds like a balanced and reasonable position, halfway between the poles as it were, Chakrabarti's language certainly tips her toward the salvific end of the spectrum. Human rights are what people in some parts of the world "dream" of. They "empower the vulnerable." They "irritate and inconvenience the mighty." One wonders whether the faint echoes of the Magnificat are accidental.

The idea of human rights as religion is not a new or controversial one. In the words of the historian Samuel Moyn, "Christianity is the global faith that many would like human rights to become."

126

In the mind of some, there is nothing aspirational about this. It is reality. Thus the solicitor and academic Anthony Julius, writing in *The Guardian* in 2010, claimed that "a human rights discourse now dominates politics; there is a powerful human rights 'movement.' It is the new secular religion of our time."

Some take this a step further, contending that if human rights is the liberal West's new orthodoxy, it must come at the expense of the old one. According to the human rights lawyer Francesca Klug, rights and, in particular, their incarnation in the Human Rights Act are our *Values for a Godless Age*. More antagonistically, the columnist Deborah Orr wrote in 2013 that "for human rights to flourish, religious rights have to come second to them."

It is worth pondering such simplistic pronouncements. Deborah Orr seems to be unaware of the fact that religious rights are human rights, both legally and philosophically; or that there is no algorithm to judge between which human rights take precedence when; or that there is not—and could never be—a preordained set of priorities that established a permanent and inflexible hierarchy between different human rights, as to do so would be to subordinate some rights to secondary status in such a way as effectively to devalue them entirely. Such quibbles notwithstanding, views such as Orr's are not uncommon.

On account of their alleged origins, rights are often judged as somehow incompatible, in competition, or at the very least in tension with Christianity. More precisely, this view rests on two distinct narratives about the roots of rights: philosophical and political.

The first contends that the ideology of rights was built rather like the walls of Jerusalem after the Babylonian exile, only in this version it is Immanuel Kant who plays the role of Nehemiah, his philosophical disciples that of the returned Jews, and the Church that plays Sanballat, Tobiah, and their allies, first mocking, then plotting against, and then threatening to destroy the entire project. According to this story, it is only the deontological foundations sunk so deeply by Kant, which make an absolute and non-negotiable duty of respecting the rational nature of human beings, that can secure the walls with sufficient robustness. Admittedly, the *anti*-Christian slant of this tale is sometimes harder to justify, given Locke's role of John the Baptist to Kant's Jesus, and Kant's own pietistic upbringing in his notably holy family. Nevertheless, Kant's self-evidently lukewarm Christianity—agnosticism in all but name—and his non-theological reasoning serve to spin a story that is sufficiently non-Christian for those who wish to divorce Christianity from rights.

The second narrative is, as it were, the political sequel to this philosophical blockbuster. Rights find their political voice in the French Revolution, albeit with language developed in the previous generation by philosophical radicals. The open atheism of most of these radicals, and the Revolution's anti-Christian and, in particular, anticlerical credentials, need no emphasis—although the (Catholic) Church's relentless opposition to anything that could trace its roots back to the Revolution, rights included, over the following century offers just such an emphasis. Rights became the flag to which the secular rallied whenever the forces of religious reaction threatened oppression.

This chapter acknowledges that while there is something to be said for both of these views, especially the second, the picture is more complicated than that, and that two recent publications in particular—Nicholas Wolterstorff's *Justice: Rights and Wrongs* and Samuel Moyn's *Christian Human Rights*—offer a counternarrative to which we should pay attention if we wish to represent the full nature of Christianity's engagement with human rights.

The "conflict thesis" between science and religion, discussed elsewhere in this book, which argued that science and religion were somehow necessarily at war with one another, has been replaced by historians of science, in particular John Hedley Brooke, not by its opposite—some kind of harmony thesis, which imagines the two have always been the best of friends—but by what Brooke has termed a "complexity thesis," the straightforward idea that relations between the two have been complex, marked by moments and periods of mutual hostility and mutual support, conflict and harmony. As with science and religion, this chapter contends, so with Christianity and rights.

2

Nicholas Wolterstorff's central contention in *Justice: Rights and Wrongs* is that justice is constituted not of "right" but of "rights."

The Christian ethicist Oliver O'Donovan has remarked that this distinction might remind readers a little of the passage in Book 2 of *Decline and Fall of the Roman Empire*, where Edward Gibbon shows how the great Christological battles of the fourth century turned on a single letter: were God and Jesus *homoousios*, meaning of the same substance, or were they *homoiousios*, meaning of a similar substance? To those less enmeshed in such theological subtleties, such as Gibbon, the difference appears insignificant and facile, a fact aided in as far as the two words differ by one letter, the *iota*, which happens to be the smallest in the Greek alphabet. This is angels dancing on splinters of pin heads.

Is not the question of whether justice is based on *right* or *rights* similarly pedantic? Even if the context is more concrete—is it right that the hungry are fed or do the hungry have a right to food?—the difference is still paper thin: the hungry will get fed, or not, either way. As Wolterstorff points out, however, there is something more profound at stake here. "The debate at bottom is over the deep structure of the moral universe: what accounts for what." Do rights come from justice or does justice come from rights? Or, put another way, are rights, such as they can be said to exist, natural or are they socially or politically conferred?

There are many prominent Christian ethicists who incline to the latter but, contrary to their views, Wolterstorff argues that inherent, natural rights are not a modern invention, dating from either the eighteenth, seventeenth, or fourteenth century depending on your historical taste, but rather can be traced back to the canon lawyers of middle ages, the Church Fathers, Roman jurists, and, before them all, the Bible.

Drawing on the work of the medieval scholar Brian Tierney and his student Charles Reid, Wolterstorff argues that the language and logic of rights are readily identifiable in the legal systems of thirteenth-century Europe. Indeed, in Tierney's words, twelfth-century European society was "saturated with a concern for rights . . . mediaeval people first struggled for survival; then they struggled for rights." Thus one Godfrey of Fontaine writing in the 1280s could say, apparently without saying anything remarkable:

each one is bound by the law of nature to sustain his life, which cannot be done without exterior goods, therefore also by the law of nature each has dominion and a certain right in the common exterior goods of this world which right also cannot be renounced.

A similar point could be made of the Roman jurists and the Church Fathers nearly a millennium earlier. Even if the precise vocabulary wasn't there, the idea of natural rights clearly hovers in the background of some patristic sermons. Wolterstorff quotes examples from John Chrysostom, Ambrose of Milan, and Basil of Caesarea, who proclaimed:

that bread which you keep, belongs to the hungry; that coat which you preserve in your wardrobe, to the naked; those shoes which are rotting in your possession, to the shoeless; that gold which you have hidden in the ground, to the needy. Wherefore, as often as you were able to help others, and refused, so often did you do them wrong.

This is powerful stuff, although it seems to me an exaggeration to claim, as Wolterstorff does, that it is "as decisive as evidence in intellectual history ever gets." It is precisely the rhetorical power of Basil's words that seems to me to blunt the philosophical force of Wolterstorff's case for natural rights among the Church Fathers; Basil is pleading, shaming, exhorting his audience, all the time performing on Matthew 25. His objective, it seems to me, is to open their eyes to (what would one day be called) the universal destination of goods, a concept as consonant with "justice as right" as it is with "justice as rights." It is not that such exhortations are incompatible with the idea of natural rights. It is rather that they are equivocal.

A similar point might be made of the biblical material that stands behind such Church Fathers. This seems an even harder claim, and Wolterstorff himself recognizes that "when one attends to the prominence of divine legislation in Israel's life, everything points to the conclusion that we are dealing with a right order way of thinking." However, he proceeds to argue that the prophets and the psalmist do not argue the case that alleviating the plight of the lowly is required by justice. They assume it: "they take for granted that justice requires alleviating the plight of the lowly."

The reason for this, and indeed the Old Testament's obsessive focus on the widows, orphans, resident aliens, and poor, is that God holds his people accountable for doing justice in a highly personal way. Failing to do so is to fail in obligations to God himself, to wrong God, to deprive him of that to which he has a *right*.

If one acknowledges this—that God, in effect, has rights—one has made a crucial move toward recognizing natural human rights. "To think of human beings as having inherent rights it to think of human beings as little gods, sovereign individuals." But that, of course, is precisely how Scripture does envisage humans, bearing his image, imitating his nature, discharging his role on earth. In other words, it is from God's natural right as God that humans acquire natural rights as humans. Thus "the proscription against murder is grounded not in God's law but in the worth of the human being. All who bear God's image possess, on that account, an inherent right not to be murdered."

This, Wolterstorff recognizes, is not a fully formed doctrine of inherent natural rights but, rather, the raw material for later thinkers to develop just that. It is also, I suggest, vulnerable to the same criticism levelled at Basil's exhortation. Recognizing in every human being the fact that he or she belongs to and is in relationship with God, however (un)acknowledged or broken that may be, is certainly compatible with a rights-based understanding of the moral universe. But the undeniable biblical register is one of moral exhortation directed at those who are called to respond, follow, and obey God and his commands, which rather orientates one toward a right order form of thinking.

The sense, in other words, is that the biblical material can be used to derive a framework or foundation for natural rights, but it doesn't do so necessarily. There is equivocation within Scripture born not least of its exhortative, rhetorically charged, and often urgent genres.

3

To move from the theo-philosophical case for rights to the theo-political one is not so much to change tunes as to move from one movement of a symphony to another: themes, motifs, patterns are recognizable even if the melody and key are clearly different.

However much Wolterstorff's case for a Christian grounding of human rights might be legitimate, it wasn't shared by European

Christians of the modern period. For all the early modern period pondered rights, in the wake of the conquest of the Americas and the questions that raised about the rights of indigenous tribes, they came of age in the Enlightenment, and in particular with the American and French Revolutions and their respective declarations of Independence and of the Rights of Man. Rights were not only, it seemed, quintessentially modern but associated with an anti-authoritarianism that, predictably, the Churches rejected.

This changed in the early decades of the twentieth century and in particular from the 1930s. In 1925, the Catholic philosopher Jacques Maritain drew the distinction between person and individual when discussing what he took to be modernity's wrong turn, which he laid at the door of Luther, Descartes, and Rousseau. In doing so, he was recapturing the Thomistic idea of the person, as someone distinct and inherently relational. At the time, those who were setting out on this path were more likely to find themselves favoring authoritarian regimes over liberal alternatives, as these placed heavy rhetorical emphasis on the importance of community and seemed a viable refuge from the horrors of the communistic and materialistic view of human nature in the East and the individuated and atomistic vision of the liberal West. Maritain himself was still involved with the far-right movement Action Française at the time, although he abandoned them when they were condemned by the Church for nationalistic and anti-democratic tendencies the following year.

Personalism thereafter began to find its feet independent of statist and nationalist ideologies. A personalist political manifesto was issued in 1931 from the rightist club the Ordre Nouveau, but was explicitly not collectivist—nor, of course, individualist—in its emphasis. Personalism's strength was arguably in its indeterminacy. Maritain claimed that there were at least a dozen different personalist doctrines that he knew about, and even communism tried to get in on the game in around 1934. It was Maritain himself, however, who helped provide a more substantial analysis, moving it emphatically away from authoritarianism and defending "a pluralism founded on the dignity of the human person, and established on the basis of complete equality of civic rights, and effective respect for the liberties of the person in his individual life." By means of such re-evaluation the movement gained momentum during the mid-1930s, aided in no small measure by the dawning realization that far-right parties in Spain, Italy, and in particular Germany might have offered a refuge from communism but did so now at too great a cost. Personalism became a narrow and vulnerable path between two ideological heresies, and human dignity became a bulwark against the sins of both.

Moyn puts forward 1937 as the key turning point in this story, for two reasons. First, it was in that year that a new Irish Constitution was drawn up. The Preamble to this began, "In the Name of the Most Holy Trinity, from Whom all authority and to Whom, as our final end, all actions both of men and States must be referred," and continued on to use the words, "seeking to promote the common good, with due observance of Prudence, Justice and Charity, so that the dignity and freedom of the individual may be assured." Moyn observes that the term "dignity" had been used before then. Papal encyclicals, for example, such as the important *Quadragesimo anno* of 1931, had used the term when attached to collective entities like workers or to religious sacraments like marriage. There was, however, little precedent for it being used of human beings and in this particular way. The Irish Constitution was groundbreaking, marking the emergence of constitutional dignity, causing the Vatican newspaper *L'Osservatore Romano* to remark that "it differs from other Constitutions because it is inspired by respect for the faith of the people, the dignity of the person, the sanctity of the family, or private property, and of social democracy."

As it happens, and in spite of this, the future Pius XII had some problems with the Constitution as it did not recognize the Catholic Church as the one true Church, but he was nonetheless satisfied with it, not least because his predecessor, Pius XI, who had been on the throne of Peter in 1937, had issued several encyclicals, such *Mit brennender Sorge* (on the Church and the German Reich) and *Divini redemptoris* (on atheistic communism), which had highlighted the significance of human dignity. These constitute the second reason for highlighting 1937. Communism, Pius proclaimed in the latter encyclical, "strips man of his liberty, [and] robs human personality of all its dignity." It "denies the rights, dignity and liberty of human personality." The encyclical strikes the personalist balance between collective responsibility and unencumbered individual freedom . . .

> it is impossible to care for the social organism and the good of society
> as a unit unless each single part and each individual member—that is
> to say, each individual man in the dignity of his human personality—is
> supplied with all that is necessary for the exercise of his social functions

. . . in such a way as would make the idea of rights tenable in the 1940s.

The alliance between human dignity and rights was still a very tenuous one, however, and it was not until halfway through the Second World War that the two became more closely and firmly associated. American Catholic bishops used the language of rights in 1942, as did German bishops in a pastoral letter of Easter 1942 when they complained against the Nazi regime and "the general rights divinely guaranteed to men." The French Catholic resistance group Témoignage Chrétien republished and amplified it in a 1942 booklet, "Human and Christian Rights." Maritain himself was increasingly campaigning on the issue and published *The Rights of Man and Natural Law* in 1942, in which he said, "The dignity of the human person . . . means nothing if it does not signify that by virtue of natural law, the human person has the right to be respected, is the subject of rights, possesses rights." Most influentially, which is where Moyn's book actually begins, Pope Pius XII's Christmas message of 1942 firmly and explicitly—and very publicly—associated dignity and rights in a way that now became hard to avoid.

From having been a secular and liberal idea, rights came to be seen by the notably more conservative Catholic Church as a bulwark against a hyperactive and overbearing state, especially when that state was communistic, as well as against the secularism, materialism, and relativism that it felt threatened to undermine common order. However else it might be read, this growth of rights talk was not secular. In Moyn's words:

> Historians who have examined the crucial early war years to trace
> the rise of the hitherto largely unused phrase (in English) of "human
> rights" have discovered only minor percolations until something
> happened to bring the term into its immediate post-war moment of
> increased use. Completely neglected among these percolations . . . is
> the comparatively early Catholic articulation of the human rights idea.

If conservative Christian thought bore the language and logic of human rights in the immediate pre-war and war years, it was generally conservative Christian thinkers and parties that nurtured it in the post-war period.

Maritain continued as an effective global evangelist for human rights, both in UNESCO and as French ambassador to the Holy See, where he helped orientate Pope Pius XII toward human rights language in the late 1940s. Charles Malik, a Lebanese Christian, was responsible for the personalistic language in the UN Declaration itself. In Moyn's words, "the human person became a key figure in thought at the United Nations, thanks to Christians who were impressed by papal language and who injected it into founding documents."

In Europe, the post-war dominance of Christian democracy secured the future of human rights there. Christian democracy is little discussed in Anglophone circles. Moyn points out that Tony Judt's massive history, *Postwar: A History of Europe since 1945*, has almost nothing to say about it. However, it was almost hegemonic in the 1950s and '60s. Post-war constitutions of rehabilitated nations adopted the idea and the language of human rights, starting with the Bavarian Constitution of 1946, the Italian Constitution of 1947, and the Basic Law for the Federal Republic of Germany in 1949. Even the preamble to the French Constitution of 1947, never likely to be a good place to find language that had been baptized by the Catholic Church, mentioned the human person (though not, naturally, God, or even human dignity). More broadly, the founders of the European project were Christian democratic politicians steeped in personalistic thought, such as the French prime minister Robert Schuman, the German chancellor Konrad Adenauer, the Italian prime minister Alcide De Gasperi, and Pierre-Henri Teitgen, the president of the Christian Democratic Party in France in the early 1950s. All in all, at least until the 1960s, it was Christian-inspired or at least Christian-flavored parties and movements that were responsible for the embedding of human rights within European and even global politics.

4

This chapter, like this volume, has been careful not to slip quietly from historical to normative claims. It is one thing to argue that human rights have been philosophically or politically grounded in Christian thought and activity; it is quite another to say that they therefore must be and, by implication, to claim that if we continue to see the melancholy, long, withdrawing roar of faith in certain parts of the world, Europe most obviously, we will lose our commitment to human rights.

Wolterstorff does make the case—indeed it occupies a sizeable proportion of his book—that only Christian theism can successfully ground a commitment to human rights. He goes through a number of alternatives, focusing on the Kantian approach, which is undoubtedly the most serious alternative (not to mention the most significant philosophical influence on the development of human rights in the modern era). However, he concludes that

> the fatal flaw in Kant's capacities approach [is that] if we insist that the capacity for rational agency gives worth to all and only those who stand to the capacity in the relation of actually possessing it, then it is not *human* rights that are grounded but the rights of those who possess the capacity.

By contrast, he says, the Christian basis sidesteps any capabilities trap:

> if God loves equally and permanently each and every creature who bears the *imago dei*, then the relational property of being loved by God is what we have been looking for. Bearing that property gives to each human being who bears it the worth in which natural human rights inhere.

There is undoubtedly something in this argument: unless one recognizes something wholly alien or "given" or sacred when one comes into contact with another human, it is hard to see how you can ground inalienable dignity. Put another way, if human dignity is grounded in something humans do or possess, then it is contingent on their being able to do or possess it. The Christian grounding of human rights has the advantage of being grounded in something entirely other, beyond human control—or indeed comprehension.

Even if one believes that Christian faith does indeed ground human rights more satisfactorily than other alternatives, however, there is still the question of whether such a grounding is really necessary. The story of the Universal Declaration of Human Rights is a good example in this regard. As already noted, the Declaration is saturated with the language of personalism. The Preamble begins by recognizing "the inherent dignity and the equal and inalienable rights of all members of the human family" as "the foundation of freedom, justice and peace in the world," and goes on to talk about the "faith" that the peoples of the United Nations have in "the dignity and worth of the human person and in the equal rights of men and women." Article 2 talks of "the right to life, liberty and security of person" and Article 6 of "the right to recognition everywhere as a person before the law." Article 22 states that "everyone … is entitled to realization … of the economic, social and cultural rights indispensable for his dignity and the free development of his personality"; Article 26(2) states that education "shall be directed to the full development of the human personality and to the strengthening of respect for human rights" and Article 29(1) that "everyone has duties to the community in which alone the free and full development of his personality is possible."

The personalistic hinterland here is about as clear as it is possible to be, but even if one can see the hand of Malik or Maritain hovering in the background, one cannot avoid the fact that the Declaration is not a personalistic document. Indeed, it conspicuously fails to justify its faith in human dignity or, rather, does so only in negative, historically specific, or aspirational terms. Thus the Preamble declares how "disregard and contempt for human rights have resulted in barbarous acts which have outraged the conscience of mankind" and how "if man is not to be compelled to have recourse, as a last resort, to rebellion against tyranny and oppression, that human rights should be protected by the rule of law." Similarly, it speaks of the "advent" of a world in which "human beings shall enjoy freedom of speech and belief and freedom from fear and want," which has been "proclaimed as the highest aspiration of the common people." As observed in an earlier chapter, Maritain subsequently remembered that at one of the meetings of a UNESCO National Commission where human rights were being discussed, "someone expressed astonishment that certain champions of violently opposed ideologies had agreed on a list of those rights. 'Yes,' they said, 'we agree about the rights but on condition that no one asks us why.'"

If that worked for the Declaration then, why is it not an option now? This is not an altogether silly suggestion. After all, most of us do what most of us do through largely unreflective habits and instincts. Digging down deep and searching hard for secure foundations for

137

dignity and rights is perhaps to return to Gibbon's iota. But while not being silly it is perhaps a little complacent. We may well behave by habit and instincts but our habits and instincts are still shaped by ideas, albeit over periods of time that are too long for most of us to notice. Moreover, as the legal scholar Christopher McCrudden has noted, "with the increased political salience of human rights, and the increased use in litigation of human rights language, has come increasing attention on the theoretical underpinnings of human rights." The more weight we pile on the edifice the more reason we have to ascertain how it might sway or buckle. Perhaps most tellingly, when respected ethicists makes serious arguments about the non-human status of mentally disabled infants, medical ethicists make sincere cases for infanticide (or post-natal termination, as they euphemistically call it), and advanced Western democracies legislate for the euthanasia of children, one can see the thread of equal, permanent, incommensurable dignity for all humans fraying.

Shami Chakrabarti's book, with which we began, is not apocalyptic about human rights and nor, hopefully, is this chapter. However, her and Liberty's ongoing vigilance is itself a good reason to guard against undue complacency. Christianity cannot claim to be human rights' savior, riding in on its white charger just as it appears to be swallowed up in some relativistic swamp. Given the distinctly checkered and chilly relationship the two have had, that would be as false a reading of the history and future as those who imagine that human rights is a kind of anti-Christian movement. But it is perhaps precisely because of that checkered, or complex, relationship that it is worth integrating serious Christian theological reflection when thinking about the foundation and future for human rights. If, as Samuel Moyn says, "no one interested in where human rights came from can afford to ignore Christianity," we might want to say the same about where human rights are going.

10

The Secular Self

————•◦•————

The story of the secularization of the West is, according to received wisdom, a 500-year-long intellectual striptease act. Once upon a time Europeans, like every other culture round the world, were clothed in a collection of more or less fantastical and alluring beliefs, fineries like immortality, the soul, cosmic justice, human uniqueness and purpose, the supernatural realm, and so forth. Over the ensuing centuries these were gradually discarded, sometimes willingly, more often not, until at some point in the twentieth century we found ourselves standing naked.

Ultimately, the argument goes, we are all the same once we have discarded the threadbare spiritual garments we clung to in order to keep out the cold of reality and embraced the metaphysical nakedness that is our natural state. Moreover, we discover that once we have done this we find that we all, equally naturally, hold to the same values—of individualism, autonomy, liberty, tolerance, and equality—with which all reasonable people naturally agree. Purpose and eternal destiny may be gone, but we need not be ashamed of what that leaves us with. Indeed, we should really be proud of it—of, as philosopher Charles Taylor puts it, "this sense of ourselves as beings both frail and courageous, capable of facing a meaningless, hostile universe without faintness of heart, and of rising to the challenge of devising our own rules of life."

This is the thesis, more formally termed the "subtraction" theory, that leads us naturally toward "exclusive humanism," which Charles Taylor counters in his magnum opus *A Secular Age*. His topic is a familiar one, tracing an intellectual journey that takes us—by which he essentially means those of us shaped by Western ideas—from a society in which it was virtually impossible not to believe in God, "to one in which faith, even for the staunchest believer, is one human possibility among others."

Belief for Taylor is not something that goes on only from the neck upwards, a detached cerebral activity that is about which facts concerning the world we think are true and which facts we think are false. Belief and non-belief are, for him, not theories but "different kinds of lived experience involved in understanding your life in one way or the other." In other words, they are as much about living as they are about thinking.

This is important because as soon as you have reduced religious faith to a set of propositions about the existence of God or the soul or eternity, you have lost the plot, guilty not only of treating it as something it is not but, more importantly, as something it has never been. The story of the secularization of the West is not simply the tale of how we came to abandon some propositions in favor of others but of how we have come to see the world and live in it differently. It is a story of selves and the worlds, or "imaginaries," that they create. Taylor's is a study of "the whole context in which we experience and search for fullness," and in particular of the shift from "a world in which the place of fullness was understood as unproblematically outside of or 'beyond human life,' to a conflicted age in which this construal is challenged by others which place it . . . 'within human life.'"

That the modern West discovered the "immanent order of Nature," whose working could be systematically understood and explained in its own terms, is not in doubt. What is left open to question is whether this whole order has any deeper significance, and what that may or may not mean for humans. A secular age is one in which the idea that the true goal of existence lies in immediate human flourishing and not one in which "seeking, or acknowledging, or serving a good which is beyond" becomes conceivable, and in some cases seemingly obligatory. Its emergence is a tale of moral and social "imaginaries" rather than dust-ups about miracles and the supernatural. And it is also an evolutionary tale. "The straight path of modern secularity can't be sustained," Taylor remarks early on (well, on page 95, although that still counts as early in a book of 800 pages). "What I'm offering . . . is a zig-zag account, one full of unintended consequences."

2

Taylor begins around the year 1500, in an enchanted world, populated by spirits both good and bad. In this world, power—genuine causal and spiritual power—and meaning were to be found in things as well as in people, and the line between inner personal agency and outer impersonal force was not clearly drawn. There was, in effect, a "porous boundary" between the mind and the world, between the moral and the physical (hence the association of sin and illness). The porous human self was, and certainly felt, vulnerable.

In this world, God was the protector and guarantor of order and the Church's good magic kept the devil's dark magic at bay, a fact that helps explain the seriousness with which our late-medieval ancestors took heresy, which otherwise looks like the model of vindictive pettiness. To believe wrongly in this world, let alone to disbelieve altogether, was to threaten to detune the entire cosmos, or at least to remove God's ongoing protection against the powers of chaos and disorder. In this world, unbelief was not only inconceivable; it was positively dangerous, an act not so much of intellectual rebellion as social terrorism.

This world view began to change, as everything else did, with the Reformation. So vast and all-encompassing were the intellectual changes of the sixteenth century that there are innumerable strands that Taylor might have chosen to follow here. But his fresh and compelling preferred strand lies in what he calls, in another of his slightly idiosyncratic but powerful terms, the move toward a "buffered self."

The "buffered self" was the self that was separated and insulated from the rest of the world, erecting a boundary between the human mind as agent and any others that might exist. One effect of the Reformation was to disenchant the world, and the Church, in such a way as to reduce its capacity for agency, making the buffered self possible in a way that it could not have been amid the more "animated" creation of previous centuries. Sixteenth-century men and women could, of course, be as superstitious as their medieval grandparents— indeed, given their often hysterical reaction to the tumultuous affairs of their age they were arguably more so—but the principle had shifted. The first tentative steps toward a mechanized world picture were being taken and, as Peter Harrison and others have shown, thinkers were increasingly inclined not to read divine signs from earthly creatures so much as to understand, and instrumentalize, them on their own terms. Agency was relocated from having been everywhere to lying solely within the human mind. The self was fortified against an unpredictable and threatening cosmos that was itself gradually becoming marginally less unpredictable and threatening.

3

It was by means of the creation of this buffered self that the model of godliness, of the truest human good, began to shift. In place of the withdrawn, contemplative ascetic of the middle ages, the early modern period came to prize the active, controlled, responsible citizen. Ordinary life was sanctified and society placed unprecedented emphasis on disciplined sexual morality, strict poor laws, schooling and education, industry, productivity, and prosperity, all of which served as marks of holiness. Human agency was active and constructive and efficacious. A Reformed world view did not imagine or want to remake the world in man's image, but it did imagine that the world could be remade. Buffered selves had the capacity, and the responsibility, to do so.

A disciplined personal life helped create a well-ordered or "disciplinary" society, and in the process helped generate an important modification in the conception of the state. The starting point here had been an essentially Augustinian understanding in which the earthly powers existed to keep some kind of order within a fallen world but recognized their limitations and, in particular, the fact that the job of imparting virtue lay beyond their powers and brief. In this world the state could—and should—repress heresy and support the Church, as that was a legitimate part of resisting evil, but only the Church could actually inculcate goodness. However much it might seem otherwise, the role was fundamentally negative rather than positive.

The early Reformers vastly increased the powers of the magistrate, seeking in particular princes the power to cement their evangelical faith. At the same time, they rigorously dematerialized the Church, thereby removing the single biggest obstacle to untrammelled "secular" power that the middle ages had seen. It was thus something of an embarrassment when Reformed scholars later in the sixteenth century, finding themselves needing to justify political resistance toward leaders who turned out to be less pliable or faithful than they had hoped, ended up turning to Catholic theories of resistance to do so. Such tortuous hypocrisies notwithstanding, however, the political shift generated the idea of the kind of Christian state that could—and should—do much more than keep order; whose remit was positive and concerned with personal virtue.

This radical shift in agency, locating so much potential within the human mind as opposed to the natural or supernatural worlds, inevitably ended up shaping what was sought as well as how it was sought. In effect, the greater recognition of the self as agent animated recognition of the self as end. What increasingly motivated people was "no longer a sense of being in tune with nature, our own and/or that in the cosmos [but] . . . something more like the sense of our own intrinsic worth: something clearly self-referential." The final human good was not necessarily in following God, let alone glorifying him, but in seeking a good that was immanent and self-evident.

4

This didn't necessarily cut God out of the picture altogether—after all, the power to achieve these immanent ends might in some sense come from God—but it did push him toward the periphery. The world was still clearly designed by God but there was a dramatic "narrowing of the purposes of Divine Providence." God's goals for humans shrank to the single end of enabling us to achieve our own good. Moreover, the mechanical turn in natural philosophy meant that there was an accompanying shift toward an impersonal order of creation. God related to buffered, disciplined selves, in as far as he did at all, primarily "by establishing a certain order of things, whose moral shape we can easily grasp, if we are not misled by false and superstitious notions." The sense that God was planning a transformation of human beings, "which would take them beyond the limitations which inhere in their present condition," was abandoned. The "very scrutability" of creation left little room for mystery. "What Calvin did to the mysteries of the Catholic Church, Toland did to mystery as such," as a result of which religion narrowed to moralism and elided with happiness as duty and self-interest coalesced.

God remained creator, and his general—as opposed to his particular—interest in humans remained a definite possibility. Humans should be grateful for providence, as God has designed our good and laid out the potential for its achievement, albeit it was now us who were increasingly responsible for detecting and delivering it. In a nice example of unintended consequences, Taylor points out that Kant was highly influential in this process, in spite of the continuing place of God and immortality in his system, because he articulated so strongly the power of inner sources of morality. God might be there, but if the moral engine of transformation lay within, and the object of transformation could be self-determined, he didn't have much to do. The buffered self, "capable of disciplined control and benevolence, generated its own sense of dignity and power, [and] its own inner satisfactions," and these in turn led in the direction of the "exclusive humanism" that would become ever more credible in the modern world.

5

It was as a result of these fundamental transformations—from the porous to the buffered self, from ubiquitous agency to highly concentrated, from the twin-track contemplative society of the middle ages to the unified "disciplinary" one of the Reformation period—that many of the features of the modern secular world as we recognize it emerged. Taylor emphasizes three, in the economy, the practices and outlooks of democratic self-rule, and the public sphere.

The idea, as Alexander Pope put it, that "true SELF-LOVE and SOCIAL are the same" underlay the first. The "social imaginary" shifted from society as an organized body, with certain established functions set in a permanent and largely inflexible hierarchy, to society as a self-organizing market, an area of human exchange in which self-interest invariably led to the optimal collective results.

The brief of governance, having, as noted, been vastly extended in the sixteenth century, was curtailed, in some areas, in the eighteenth by the growing belief, albeit among elite minorities, that the self that could determine its own ends needed to grant its consent for authority to be legitimate. This might have been a distinctly Christian doctrine in its early incarnations, as John Locke's resolutely biblical "First Treatise on Government" shows, but it didn't appear to be necessarily Christian, as those American Founding Fathers, who idolized Locke but were determinedly deistic in their religious persuasions, illustrated.

In much the same way, the public square—defined by Taylor as a common space in which the members of society come together through a variety of media to discuss matters of common interest and are thus able to form a common mind in response—becomes not only possible but necessary if these selves are to be well served. No longer was public discussion necessarily political or ecclesiastical. There now existed a realm in which selves, unencumbered by religious or political authority and office, might come together and discuss their common life, without the permission of government or Church.

Through such developments the idea of the sovereign people emerged, a concept "taken out of mythical time" and relocated to the present, large-scale social transformation now becoming something that could be brought about by collective action in contemporary, purely secular time. The "crucial fiction" of "we, the people," as a real, legitimate, and efficient agent was born. Revolutions from the American onwards might still be tinged with retrospection—the American revolutionaries still claimed to be seeking to secure traditional rights of free Englishmen—but they were no longer predicated on the attempt to recapture a golden age

From such materials the full social imaginary of "exclusive humanism" could be constructed. The buffered self, centralized agency, the disciplined society, an immanent frame for the human good: between them Westerners had enough to construct the world view with which we are familiar today.

In this world the individual not only existed—as we saw in the chapter on Larry Siedentop's *Inventing the Individual,* the concept of the individual could be traced into the soil of Christian thought and could be said to exist at least conceptually by the middle ages— but it existed as an entity that was disembedded from the rest of the cosmos and from social roles. Society could be understood as a society of individuals each pursuing his or her own ends by his or her means. This, Taylor emphasizes, was a remarkable achievement—not necessarily a wholly commendable achievement but an accomplishment nonetheless. Failing to recognize quite how unusual it is and how much effort was put into it, lies at the base of the erroneous "subtraction" theory with which we started.

> The mistake of moderns is to take this understanding of the individual so much for granted, that it is taken to be our first-off self-understanding "naturally." Just as, in modern epistemological thinking, a neutral description of things is thought to impinge first on us, and then "values" are "added"; so here, we seize ourselves first as individuals, then become aware of others, and of forms of sociality. This makes it easy to understand the emergence of modern individualism by a kind of subtraction story: the old horizons were eroded, burned away, and what emerges is the underlying sense of ourselves as individuals.

On the contrary, he emphasizes, it would be more accurate to say that our natural identity is relational or tribal and only later did we come to conceive of ourselves as free individuals. The secular self created a secular world for itself, which then became normalized in such a way as left certain moderns bewildered that there could ever be any other way of thinking and living.

6

And this is where the story *should* end. This is the conclusion of the secularization tale, the self as individuated, untethered, autonomous, free within its immanent frame, unencumbered by any impression of transcendence: a position of contented exclusive humanism, increasingly incomprehensive of, and contemptuous toward, alternatives.

The problem is that it is a conclusion that some had already reached by the later eighteenth century and which many more reached in the nineteenth and twentieth. And, rather obviously, history did not end as they reached it. More precisely, this terminus proved not to be a terminus but a junction.

Originally a clear and compelling alternative to Christianity, the development of exclusive humanism "set in train a dynamic, something like a nova effect, spawning an ever-widening variety of moral/spiritual options, across the span of the unthinkable and perhaps even beyond." Although this was limited to elites until well into the twentieth century, this "nova" effect of intellectual and spiritual pluralization became then

146

a "supernova" one—"a kind of galloping pluralism on the spiritual plane"—as there arose in Western societies "a generalized culture of 'authenticity,' or expressive individualism, in which people are encouraged to find their own way, discover their own fulfillment."

Disenchantment with disenchantment in fact began early. Pietists, Wesleyans, and evangelicals were all products of the age of reason, and although historians are increasingly alert to their positive engagement with rationalism, they nonetheless gained a certain energy and momentum from the sense that the exclusive humanism toward which rationalism was orientating people drew the compass of life too narrowly. There was more to life than this.

The critique extended way beyond these orthodox bounds, however. Indeed, its strength and historical interest—and the reason why Taylor spends so much time discussing it—lies precisely in the fact that rather than acting like a straightforward pendulum, which swung back against exclusive humanism with predictable linear force, the reaction spun off in many unprecedented directions. The Western cultural pattern moved from orderly shape, to complex pattern, to indiscernible chaos.

The inclination to reduce everything to calculation, utility, profit and loss depressed many diverse souls. In the words of Thomas Carlyle, then considered the conscience of a nation, now rarely read outside the academy, the rationalists and utilitarians were busy "reducing this God's-World to a dead brute Steam-engine, the infinite celestial Soul of Man to a kind of Hay-balance for weighing hay and thistles on, pleasures and pains on." Man could not live by Bentham alone. What was to be done?

Some sought a return to the faith from which they had once slipped, but a growing number of people, unable to accept orthodox Christianity, sought "alternative spiritual sources," Romanticism, as we now call it, being the most obvious. Beauty, Taylor writes,

> required the harmonious fusion of moral aspiration and desire, hence of reason and appetite. The accusation against the dominant conceptions of disciplined self and rational order was that they had divided these, that they had demanded that reason repress, deny feeling; or alternatively, that they had divided us, confined us in a desiccated reason which had alienated us from our deeper emotions.

147

In beauty many touched the hem of a transcendence that rationalism denied them. Kant claimed that the sight of an overwhelming power in Nature, which we could never resist, like volcanoes or waterfalls, "awakens an awareness of ourselves as noumenal beings, who stand as high above all this merely sensible reality, as within the sensible realm the threatening phenomenon stands above our puny phenomenal selves." Wordsworth put it better in his lines written above Tintern Abbey.

> And I have felt
> A presence that disturbs me with the joy
> Of elevated thoughts; a sense sublime
> Of something far more deeply interfused,
> Whose dwelling is the light of setting suns,
> And the round ocean and the living air,
> And the blue sky, and in the mind of man:

Such feelings would eventually lead back toward the orthodox Christianity that Wordsworth, unlike Coleridge, had never really escaped, but for many others it was a pathway to positions that were, in the parlance today, spiritual but not religious.

Thus, feeling forced to choose between the unpalatable that was desiccated rationalism, and the incredible that was reinvigorated Catholicism, a number of early-nineteenth-century French freethinkers developed a third way: religiosity shorn of God. The nineteenth century became the great age of credulity in France, with a relentless fascination for non-Christian and often non-theistic religious beliefs and phenomena. Neo-Platonists, gnostics, cabbalists, mystics, Rosicrucians, Swedenborgians, illuminists, freemasons, Essenes, and spiritualists multiplied, as did interest in eastern religions, and a fascination with table-turning, automatic writing, séances, magic, the paranormal, phrenology, thaumaturgy, mesmerism, somnambulism, chiromancy, and cartomancy. More substantially, if not necessarily any saner, Henri de Saint-Simon and, in his footsteps, Auguste Comte developed their Religion of Humanity, the child of which grew into the Ethical Societies of late Victorian Britain, and the grandchild into the oddly ceremonial exclusive humanism seen in the secular humanist movement today.

A third path was that of high culture, epitomized in the figure of Matthew Arnold, whose reasoning held that a society shorn of Christianity was threatened with "anarchy," which only the diffusion of high culture could combat. This was the responsibility of the "clerisy"—a learned, literary, social cabal whose very sophistication laid upon it the duty of preserving and spreading sweetness and light throughout society, thereby fighting back the various armies of barbarism that threatened civilization. Taylor observes that this was "very much like the maintenance of certain forms of worship by a national church," but it could sometimes feel, rhetorically at least, more like the Benedictine monasteries whose walled gardens nurtured what was left of civilization as the Dark Ages descended on Europe.

All the while this was happening, the universe of unbelief was expanding, not, as the popular imagination has it, because of science but for wider contextual reasons. "Materialism [was] nourished by certain ways of living in, and further developing, our cosmic imaginary; certain ways of inflecting our sense of the purposelessness of this vast universe, our awe at and sense of kinship with it." In effect, exclusive humanist selves created exclusive humanist social imaginaries that then reflected back to themselves and normalized exclusive humanist selves and imaginaries.

Some reactions within the supernova set out on still other courses, eschewing orthodoxy, spiritual heterodoxy, high culture, exclusive humanism, and sometimes, as in the case of Marxism, managing to combine seemingly irreconcilable elements by making a transcendent system out of thoroughly material material. The point, however, is less which or how many reactions there were to the intellectual genesis of exclusive humanism, or what combinations of materialism and transcendence, orthodoxy and eccentricity they exhibited, so much as the fact that there *were* reactions, an ever-growing number, which appeared to suggest that the achievement of exclusive humanism was not as self-evidently fulfilling as many at first thought. What Taylor terms a "malaise" set in around our "purely immanent humanism," a malaise that had no real precedent in history:

> You hear complaints about this "present age" all through history—that it is fickle, full of vice and disorder, lacking in greatness or high deeds,

full of blasphemy and viciousness. But what you won't hear at other times and places is one of the commonplaces of our day . . . that our age suffers from a threatened loss of meaning.

We suffer from a malaise of immanence, a "felt flatness of our attempts to solemnize the crucial moments of passage in our lives" (witnessed by the attempt of exclusive humanist organizations to establish celebrants and to formalize funeral ceremonies and the like). Having arrived at the secular self, we kept on searching. We still are.

7

"Our age is very far from settling in to a comfortable unbelief," Taylor remarks toward the end. The sociologist Steve Bruce's imagined end-point for human history, "not self-conscious irreligion . . . [but] widespread indifference," strikes Taylor as being "deeply implausible." Not only are there vast areas of the industrializing, modernizing world that are not secularizing as was once confidently predicted, but even in Western strongholds of the secular self, pressures exist. "The secular age is schizophrenic, or better, deeply cross-pressured." For all those milieux in which "unbelief is close to being the default solution (including important parts of the academy)," there are many that remain fascinated and fixated by the beyond.

Either way, wherever one turns, "moral self-authorization" dominates, a state in which ever more people believe that authentic self-expression is the only right way to live. In some regards this is the antipathy to the disciplined self of the post-Reformation period. We are undergoing an "expressive revolution" in which "choice" is deemed "an all-trumping argument." The result is that when individuals do react against the constraints of exclusive humanism, they do so in a now bewildering range of diffuse, individuated, disembedded ways, creating an unprecedented "new spiritual landscape." Taylor's own view, which he freely confesses is shaped by his own perspective "as a believer," is that

> the salient feature of the modern cosmic imagery is not that it has
> fostered materialism, or enabled people to receive a spiritual outlook
> beyond materialism, to return as it were to religion, though it has done
> both of those things . . . [but that] it has opened a space in which people

can wander between and around all these options without having to land clearly and definitely in any one.

There is, he concludes, no long-term movement toward a resolution of any kind. Both those "who hope that unbelief will encounter its own unbelief and aridity, and will peter out in a general return to orthodoxy," and their opponents, who "think that all this represents a historic march towards reason and science, seem doomed to disappointment."

Hence talk of post-secular Europe is not intended to indicate that orthodox religion is surging back from the long-distant shoreline, or that the number of religiously disengaged is reversing. Neither seems imminently likely. Rather, it is that there remains a palpable sense that the secular self isn't enough, that it doesn't satisfy. There are those who disagree, and tend to do so vociferously, but they often do so from a sample size of one or two like-minded individuals, convinced that the plural of anecdote is data.

Real data suggest otherwise. When, in 2012–13, Theos conducted a series of research surveys about Church of England cathedrals, the results showed that, rather than gratefully sloughing off their spiritual weeds when they found themselves in a cathedral, the non-religious often wriggled out of their secular selves. "The cathedral gives me a greater sense of the sacred than I get elsewhere," according to over half of church non-attenders who had actually visited one in the previous twelve months. Even among self-identifying secular tourists—that is, those who came to cathedrals self-consciously as tourists, as opposed to as pilgrims or worshippers—a large proportion was sensitive to some kind of spiritual experience: 84 percent of them still agreed with the idea that they got a sense of the sacred from the cathedral building, 79 percent that they got a sense of the sacred from the cathedral music, and 56 percent that they experienced God through the calm and the quiet of the cathedral space. In-depth interviews confirmed and added color. "What is important is the ability the cathedral has to make people slow down for a minute and ponder," one non-Christian businessman remarked.

> It allows you to think about others, to think about yourself, about things like guilt and the welfare of others—all of which come back to

having faith in something . . . It's about faith, not religion—it doesn't force you to believe in God or believe in the Bible . . . It instills faith in people—allowing people to make up their own minds.

As his sentiments suggest, this is a very long way from any recognizable religious faith; indeed, it remains self-consciously in tension with, almost in opposition to, religious faith, pivoting on the central and unquestioned importance of choice. But it is equally far from the satisfied secular self. While we may be unlikely to see Arnold's Sea of Faith rushing back in any time soon, Taylor concludes that "the hegemony of the mainstream master narrative" is liable to be ever more challenged as we move into the twenty-first century. "We are just at the beginning of a new age of religious searching."

11

"Always with You": Capital, *Inequality, and the "Absence of War"*

─────•◦•─────

1

At the time of writing, *Capital in the Twenty-First Century* by Thomas Piketty, a young and heretofore largely unknown economics professor, has been translated into thirty-one languages and sold over 1.5 million copies. *Capital*, as it will hereafter be referred to, is a 685-page book on macroeconomics, replete with 18 tables, 97 graphs, and 687 detailed footnotes, written originally in French and published by the respected academic publisher Belknap/Harvard. *Harry Potter and the Prisoner of Azkaban* it isn't.

These figures invite the obvious question: why? After all, it's not as if the topic on which Piketty focuses—wealth, income, and inequality—has been ignored by other economists. Better-known writers like Joseph Stiglitz, Paul Krugman, and Anthony Atkinson have all written extensively and eloquently on the topic.

Some have suggested that Piketty's success is down to his unprecedented rigor and admirable breadth. J. Bradford DeLong, a professor of economics at Berkeley, has observed that the book "combines history, quantitative estimation, social science theory, and a deep concern with societal welfare"—he might have added literature, as Jane Austen and Honoré de Balzac play frequent walk-on parts—"in a way that is too rare these days." This is true, but as he goes on to remark, that would normally make it "a book for a narrow audience: me and a few others. I expected people who did not have the souls of accountants to start to snore at Piketty's numbers, numbers, numbers and more numbers."

A more persuasive reason is surely not just that the book is thorough and the moment is right but that the argument was what people wanted to hear. According to Stephanie Kelton, Chair of the

Department of Economics at the University of Missouri–Kansas City, "it was Piketty whose meticulous examination of the evidence, seemed to provide the impartial proof audiences were craving. The left was right." Or, more pointedly still, in the words of Tyler Cowen, Professor of Economics at George Mason University, *Capital* "appears to strengthen the case for redistribution . . . If you are an activist who favors lots of redistribution, the Piketty story is a lot easier to tell yourself and to tell your audiences."

I want to argue that for all that Piketty's admirably thorough and persuasive data collection and analysis does show the left to be right—inequality is growing and market forces alone will not reverse that, largely because they cause it—the book is anything but comforting to those who seek to implement the redistributist policies of the left. It may reveal the depth of the social democratic wound, but it offers little hope of its being healed.

2

For a book of such length and depth, *Capital* can be summarized with incomparable brevity: r>g. Put slightly less gnomically, this means the average annual rate of return on capital, including profits, dividends, and other income from capital (expressed as a percentage of its total value), is greater than the rate of growth of the economy (i.e., the annual increase output). Or, in the discomforting words of the Gospel, to which we shall return, "whoever has will be given more, and they will have an abundance. Whoever does not have, even what they have will be taken from them" (Matt. 25:29 NIV).

One of *Capital's* great strengths is the masses of data on which it draws. Piketty's best sources are France and Britain, but he also looks at the USA, Germany, and to a lesser extent Japan, Italy, and Spain. In addition, anecdotally but to great effect, he draws on literature, particularly from the early nineteenth century, to depict a world in which wealth was stable (largely free from the ravages of inflation), significantly more important than income, and highly concentrated in the hands of rentiers, those who made a living from income from property or investments, and nobility, who, between them, were all but a different species from the rest of the people. If the literature helps Piketty depict this world, the data allow him to show how the arc of the universe is bending slowly back toward it.

Piketty distinguishes between three different kinds of inequality—inequality of income from labor, inequality in the ownership of capital and the income to which it gives rise, and inequality based on the interaction between these two—and this enables him to go beyond better-known measures, such as the Gini coefficient, which unhelpfully elides these distinct factors, and to analyze the problem in forensic detail.

Inequality with respect to capital, he shows, is always greater than inequality with respect to income. The top centile (1 percent's) share of capital was about 55 percent in France at the beginning of the nineteenth century, rising to 60 percent in 1880–90 and to an astonishing 70 percent on the eve of the First World War. Capital inequality was just as bad in Britain, with the top centile's share hovering between 55 percent and 60 percent over 1810–70 and rising to 70 percent in 1910 (at which time the top decile's [i.e., 10 percent's] capital share was an eye-watering 90 percent).

Virtually everywhere, the period of 1870–1914 shows a stabilization of extreme capital inequality, with data from every country for which data exist—including what would one day be the celebrated social democratic paradise of Sweden—showing the richest 10 percent of the population owning somewhere between half and virtually everything in the country. This, as Piketty notes, was the first great era of trading and financial globalization, with modern diversified capital markets, with individuals holding complex portfolios of domestic and foreign, public and private assets, all operating in a culture of unprecedented technological innovation. That may sound familiar.

Everything changed, or at least began to, in the second decade of the twentieth century. Up until then, the total national value of capital in Britain and France was around six or seven times the national income. In other words, the nation owned six times more than it earned per annum and it was therefore far easier to live well off capital than it was by working for a living. By 1950, this had fallen to two or three times. The decades between 1914 and 1945 effectively eviscerated capital and they created an age of reduced inequality that was at least as long as themselves.

This was *Les Trente Glorieuses*, as they are known in France, the "Glorious Thirty" years after the Second World War in which many Western countries experienced the happy combination of significant economic growth without exacerbating the (historically very low) levels of capital and income inequality with which they started. "For the first time in history," Piketty writes, "one could live better by obtaining a job in the top centile rather than an inheritance in the top centile: study, work, and talent paid better than inheritance." More remarkably still, growth and relative equality was combined with the rapid expansion of government activity. The combination seemed natural and right. As Piketty observes, "When incomes are increasing 5 percent a year, it is not too difficult to get people to agree to devote an increasing share of that growth to social spending." Economists and politicians came to assume that this combination of economic growth, increased public spending, and low and stable levels of inequality was the natural and inevitable direction of travel for modern societies. It wasn't.

The last decades of the twentieth century saw developed nations return slowly to the status quo ante. Growth slowed, government spending faltered, and inequality grew. By 2010, the capital/income ratio had returned close to nineteenth-century levels. Piketty shows how despite the fact that the asset *structure* of the twenty-first century has very little in common with Jane Austen's time—agricultural land has long since been replaced by buildings, business capital, and financial capital as the source of wealth—the overall *levels* and *proportions* are remarkably similar. In particular, the total value of private wealth, which stood at between two and three years' worth of national income for rich countries between 1950 and 1970, had reached between four and seven years in 2010—a remarkably strong and rapid comeback of private capital "or, to put it another way, the [re]emergence of a new patrimonial capitalism."

This naturally feeds the leftist narrative that it was the evil of Thatcherism and Reaganomics that tore up the elysian fields of social democracy that had spread through the Western world in the post-war decades. But this is not entirely right. Piketty credits the politics of the last quarter of the twentieth century with much, including "the gradual privatization and transfer of public wealth into private hands" and the determined financialization of the global economy, allowing for the total amount of financial assets and liabilities held by various sectors (including households) to increase more rapidly (in some instances considerably more rapidly) than net wealth.

But he is also clear that while *Les Trente Glorieuses* did witness significant growth, longer-term data show these were anomalous decades, years in which countries were effectively playing catch-up after the destruction of the less than glorious thirty years that preceded them. A similar logic of catch-up is dictating the rapid growth of China and India in our own time. When there is no catching up to be done, growth is naturally much lower, which means public spending becomes more difficult. As Piketty says with some finality, "there is no historical example of a country at the world technological frontier whose growth in per capita output exceeded 1.5 percent over a lengthy period of time." In other words, *Les Trente Glorieuses* would not have remained glorious even without Thatcher and Reagan.

The inequality at the end of the twentieth century was not identical to that at its start. More specifically, the emergence of what Piketty calls a "patrimonial middle class" in the post-war period, with its own wealth, prevented a return to the capital inequality levels of 1900. "We have moved from a society with a small number of very wealthy rentiers to one with a much larger number of less wealthy rentiers: a society of petits rentiers if you will." Moreover, taxation levels are, of course, very significantly higher than they were a century ago. The result is that "today one has to climb much higher in the social hierarchy before income from capital outweighs income from labor."

In addition, income inequality has become a pressing issue. The world, or at least the Anglo-Saxon world, has seen the rise of "supersalaries" in certain sectors. The vast majority of the top 0.1 percent of income hierarchy in 2000–10 in the USA consists of top managers (by comparison athletes, actors, artists, and so on make up 5 percent). As an aside, Piketty carefully but thoroughly skewers the myth that such people are worth what they are paid (see his page 335 for those who are interested in this important "debate"). If executive pay were determined by marginal productivity, as it is so often justified as being, he explains, one would expect its variance to have little to do with external variances and to depend solely or primarily on non-external variances. In fact, we observe just the opposite: it is when sales and profits increase for external reasons that executive pay rises most rapidly.

In other words, the super-paid super-execs are merely surfing good economic waves.

When he poses the key question as to whether the twenty-first century will be as unequal as the early twentieth was, Piketty puts forward some reasons to suggest that it might not. However, in spite of these and the different structure and composition of economics and inequality today, he concludes that there are no solid grounds for rejoicing, as a whole range of factors, such as state competition on taxation levels and low or even negative demographic growth, promise to make inequality of wealth increase substantially. Ultimately, the entrepreneur always turns into the rentier; it's just that in some conditions, like our own, it happens with alarming rapidity.

3

Not everywhere is or was the same in such matters, and the very fact of this difference encourages the conviction that these are political and not solely economic issues, and that they are therefore amenable to political responses. America, in particular, provides a fascinating counterpoint.

Strange as it sounds to modern ears, inequality of wealth in the USA in the nineteenth century was roughly what it was in Sweden in the 1970s. High net immigration levels, the fact that people tended to arrive with labor and not capital, and the greater availability of land encouraged economic growth and reduced the power of capital and therefore the levels of inequality. Total capital in America was less than three years' worth of income when it was six or seven in Europe.

Moreover, inequality from income was also lower in the USA than it was in Europe then. The fact that inequality in the New World seemed to be catching up with that of Old greatly worried US economists a century ago (it doesn't today, as Piketty acidly notes). Americans were worried that the nation was losing its pioneering, egalitarian spirit. Accordingly, in 1910–20 the USA established an astonishingly progressive estate tax on large fortunes, which were deemed to be incompatible with US values, as well as a progressive income tax on incomes thought to be excessive. Remarkably, to modern ears, America was the first country to raise tax rates to over 70 percent, first on income in 1919–22 and then on estates in 1937–39, in the wake of the Great Depression, for which so many Americans blamed the financiers. Astonishingly, over the period of 1932–80, the top federal income tax rate for the USA averaged 81 percent. Virtually no continental European nation ever imposed such high rates, the exceptions being Germany, in the unique circumstances of 1947–49, and the UK, which boasted an all-time peak of 98 percent in the 1970s. Over the same period the top estate tax rate in the USA remained at 70–80 percent. Of course, within the USA the picture is more complicated than this, with the relatively egalitarian North standing up against the most brutal and extreme form of inegalitarianism, namely slavery and its long economic aftermath, in the South—but the comparison with Europe for much of this period is remarkable.

The seeds of today's extreme inequality in the USA were, however, sown during this post-war period. Less physical destruction in the Second World War had a lower impact on capital than it did in Europe. In addition, the historically lower and more stable income/capital ratio perhaps explains "why Americans seem to take a more benign view of capitalism than Europeans." Either way, inequality in the USA exploded post-1980, being driven primarily by the top centile, whose share of national income rose from 9 percent in 1970s to 20 percent in the first decade of the twenty-first century. The top one-thousandth of the population have increased their share even more, from 2 percent to nearly 10 percent, while elsewhere, in France, Japan, and Sweden, for example, it stands at a "mere" 2–2.5 percent.

As with Europe, but far more so, income inequalities have reached levels of 100 years ago, though again the composition has changed, with a larger role being played by income from labor and less by capital. In the early 2010s in the USA, income from labor is about as unequally distributed as has ever been observed anywhere, Piketty notes. If trends there continue, the bottom half could earn just half as much in total remuneration as the top 10 percent by 2030.

4

Why does this matter? The first reason is that it looks set to continue. It is important to emphasize that the amount by which "r" is greater than "g" is not necessarily very much—a percentage or two a year maybe. However, by the logic of cumulative growth, it doesn't need to be very much in order to open up substantial levels of inequalities over decades. The reversion to historic low growth rates over recent decades in the West augurs capital's return, and technological progress will do little to offset this. Two hundred pages into the book, Piketty states what he calls perhaps the most important lesson of his study thus far, namely that

> modern technology still uses a great deal of capital, and . . . because capital has many uses, one can accumulate enormous amounts of it without reducing its return to zero. Under these conditions, there is no reason why capital's share must decrease over the very long run, even if technology changes in a way that is relatively favorable to labor.

Unlike in China where—for many working age currently experiencing income growth of 5–10 percent a year—wealth for the immediate future at least will come from earnings and not from savings (which are invariably inherited from much poorer parents and grandparents), Westerners are more likely to get rich from what they inherit than from what they earn, the supermanagers aside.

This goes for institutions as much as for individuals. A particularly interesting section of *Capital* analyzes the relative endowments and growths of US universities, the data for which unequivocally show that the bigger the investment, the bigger the return. "By 2100, the entire planet could look like Europe at the turn of the twentieth century, at least in terms of capital intensity." The rich will keep on getting richer.

So it matters because it seems like things are going to get worse. But it also matters, more substantively, because the consequences of growing inequality are worrying. This point has already been made often and well (while also being criticized thoroughly), most notably in Wilkinson and Pickett's *The Spirit Level*. Piketty doesn't go into their level of detail but he does enough. Significant inequality, he argues, especially of capital, "radically undermine[s] the meritocratic values on which democratic societies are based," especially when that inequality appears arbitrary. "Most people," he claims, believe that "modern growth naturally favors labor over inheritance and competence over birth." Piketty shows they are wrong and worries about what they will do if that lesson sinks in.

Of the rentier societies depicted by Balzac (and Austen), he poses the question, "under such conditions, why work? Why behave morally at all? Since social inequality was in itself immoral and unjustified, why not be thoroughly immoral and appropriate capital by whatever means are available?" The same questions apply today, only more pointedly because at least the rentier society of the early nineteenth century never pretended to be meritocratic or good.

Inequality in Balzac's time was judged to be a basic and unalterable condition of civilization, even the divine order of things: "the rich man at his castle, the poor man at his gate," and all that. Today, people are where they are not by divine fiat but (in theory) on account of the use or abuse of the properties and opportunities they had (hence the ludicrous justifications of supermanagerial supersalaries: at least Fred the Shred earned his millions, rather than inheriting them).

> Modern meritocratic society, especially in the United States, is much harder on the losers, because it seeks to justify domination on the grounds of justice, virtue, and merit, to say nothing of the insufficient productivity of those at the bottom.

These are among the relatively few moments in the book when *Capital* sounds like its more famous predecessor of the same name, and a note of Marxish apocalypse creeps in. Ongoing inequality could "lead to significant political upheaval." Such an "impoverishment of the middle class would very likely trigger a violent political reaction." "A fiscal secession of the wealthiest citizens could potentially do great damage to fiscal consent in general" (this, by the way, following on from a jaw-dropping paragraph in which Piketty shows how in most countries taxes have actually become regressive at the top of the income hierarchy). "If the tax system is not made more progressive, it should come as no surprise that those who derive the least benefit from free trade may well turn against it."

This, note, is Marxish not Marxist. Piketty admits that the great German's idea concerning the principle of infinite capital accumulation "contains a key insight" but he is otherwise quite critical, recognizing that Marx's conclusions about the collapse of capitalism were wrong, and that he had "decided on his conclusions in 1848, before embarking on the research needed to justify them." Not so, one senses, Piketty.

More to the point, and here we come to the nub of this chapter, unlike his predecessor, Piketty is very wary of economic determinism. He takes r>g to be a "historical fact, not a logical necessity." Marx's iron laws were nothing like as rigid or inevitable as he imagined. But nor, critically, were the corresponding ideas of post-war theorists, such as Simon Kuznets, that income inequality would *automatically* decrease as capitalism developed. Here, he remarks, we have simply gone from Marxist "apocalypse" to modern-day "fairy tale." There is nothing inevitable in all this.

Hence the light that so many liberals have found in Piketty's book, shining in the darkness that has not yet overcome it. Inequality is real. It is growing. It will not be solved by the market. It will not naturally disappear. But nor is it natural. It is not inevitable. It is not predestined. Rather, it is a *political* issue, and it is amenable to *political* solutions, if only the political classes—or at least their social democratic caucus— would, as Prime Minister Jim Hacker in the BBC television series *Yes, Prime Minister* once put it, grasp the nettle and take the bull by the horns.

5

This is hopeful. We ride not on iron rails of economic determinism, whether they travel to sunlit uplands of equality or down into the pit where there are a million allegedly culpable losers for every allegedly deserving winner. We are free to change the future. It is an alluring idea but there is a problem, best seen in returning to Piketty and, in particular, the middle section of his narrative arc: the period of declining but stable inequality between ca. 1914 and ca. 1974.

The brutal but unavoidable fact is that it was war that was responsible for this seismic change in inequality. Prior to the shocks of 1914–45, Piketty observes, there was no visible trend toward reduced inequality of capital ownership. "It was the wars of the twentieth century that wiped away the past to create the illusion that capitalism had been structurally transformed." Illusion is a harsh word here, but the right one.

Part—but only a limited part—of this was due to the physical destruction of capital in warfare. In Britain, Piketty estimates, physical destruction of capital due to the Second World War was less than 10 percent of national income (primarily due to bombing raids), a tenth or fifteenth of what it was in France or Germany. Nevertheless, national capital in the UK still fell by four years' worth of national income, as much as France or Germany. That was the result of politics. Simply put, *capital could be taxed or expropriated at levels previously unthinkable because the alternative was worse.* War, coming hard on the heels of a global depression widely associated with the inequality-breeding sins of global finance, created sufficient solidarity to enable the evisceration of the superrich. The post-war tax in France was, appropriately enough, called the solidarity tax.

Crucially, this continued after the fighting stopped. The shadow cast by the age of total war was a long one. Levels of income and inheritance taxation, housing prices, rent controls, coupled with demographic growth and the economic catch-up that, as we have noted, was a natural consequence of a continent renewing itself after war, meant that the post-war decades experienced whatever the opposite of a perfect economic storm is—a perfect economic calm?

Those growing up in those decades came to think this was the "new normal." People began to think of the "natural" triumph of human capital over capital in the traditional sense. Yet as *Capital* shows, it isn't. Even today the concentration of wealth has not fully recovered its pre-1914 levels, and the existence of the middle class means that it may not. But all the signs are that there is only one direction of travel.

The question is, then, if economic determinism doesn't hold all the trump cards, and if political will made manifest through progressive taxation did reduce inequality in the past, why should it not do so now? Admittedly, there are some elements from that post-war perfect economic calm—demographic growth, economic catch-up—that are just not in place for the twenty-first century West. But their absence notwithstanding, cannot politicians screw their courage to the sticking place and do the deed, whisper it: raise income taxes, make them much more progressive or even, as Piketty argues at length in the fourth and final section of the book, develop a global, or at the very least a continental, tax on capital? He—and others, including this author—hopes so, but . . . here we stumble across the fault line running under the surface of his argument, and come to "the absence of war."

David Hare's 1993 play of that name depicted the woes of a Labour leader unable to connect with the electorate (it was written in the wake of Neil Kinnock's surprise 1992 defeat, but those who read it today may call to mind a rather more recent election shock). The title's "absence of war" refers to how this generation of politicians, without ever having had to fight in a war on account of which "you have some sense of personal worth," now just seek worth by keeping busy: "We work and hope we will feel we do good."

This may well be true of contemporary politics, but there is another way the title is apposite for politics today, and specifically the *political* nature of the inequality Piketty discusses. War created not only worth but *solidarity*, an overwhelmingly powerful sense of shared interest. The presence of an "other," in particular a threatening other, often does that, and there were few more threatening others than Nazi Germany (although Soviet Russia had a not dissimilar effect on post-war European and North Atlantic politics). Put at its simplest, when the difference between us and them is that great and that terrifying, the differences between us and us shrink and, willingly or otherwise, we pool resources to secure our shared future. Inequality could be politically eviscerated during the long decades of war–depression–war because the social and cultural permission necessary for such significant political action was granted. Indeed, so strongly granted was it that it remained for decades afterwards. We did not sacrifice what we sacrificed in the war only to return to the status quo ante.

If we could do that then, then we can do so now. Eschewing ideas of rigid economic determinism, Piketty pins his hopes on democracy. One of his repeated refrains is that, once we have recognized that inequality is as much a political matter as an economic one, it becomes "a matter for democratic debate." "If we are to regain control of capitalism," he concludes in his final pages, "we must bet everything on democracy." But that is one hell of a bet. What if the people don't see things that way? "It is to be hoped that democratic deliberation will point in the right direction," he remarks on page 537.

It is to be hoped indeed but, as Piketty never quite admits, it's a hope that reaches high without ever examining the ground on which it stands. First time round, it wasn't politics that reduced inequality but *wartime* politics, the uniquely solidaristic governance made possible by uniquely shared needs and concerns. Piketty knows this. "There was no gradual, consensual, conflict-free evolution toward greater equality," he writes on page 275. "In the twentieth century it was war, and *not harmonious democratic or economic rationality*, that erased the past and enabled society to begin anew with a clean slate." Or, elsewhere: "it was war that gave rise to progressive taxation, *not the natural consequences of universal suffrage*." Or, again: "progressive taxation was as much *a product of two world wars* as it was of democracy." (All emphases added.)

To address inequality through the kinds of progressive taxation that Piketty (rightly) judges the only means of doing so, demands an overpowering sense of "us"—or common identity, or social mores, or purposes, or enemies. It requires a certain, strong, shared space of public permission in which politicians can act. The Second World War—following hard on the heels of depression and further total war—provided that in spades, revealing an alternative so ghastly that it made the demands it imposed on citizens seem slight in comparison. It cast a shadow of solidarity that lasted a generation and only then began to fade. But fade it has, and recapturing shadows is no easy task.

Without that, in "the absence of war," justifying the kind of political activity necessary to reduce inequality becomes harder. More damningly still, the kind of *petits rentiers* inequality we witness in the early twenty-first century (as opposed to the extreme and obviously obnoxious *grandes rentiers* inequality a century ago) is even more difficult to correct politically "because it is a commonplace inequality opposing broad segments of the population rather than pitting a small elite against the rest of society." It's the problem of the American Dream: powerful enough to steer people's energies into dreaming rather than campaigning. "It could be you." In the absence of war, there are insufficient centripetal forces in Western societies to justify the kind of politics needed to address inequality adequately. It seems that we will always have the poor with us.

6

Marxists liked criticizing Christians for their pessimistic determinism. It wasn't the determinism that was the problem, of course. As we have seen, economic determinism played a major role in Marxist thought. That, however, was optimistic determinism, in which the rails of history led to utopia, and not to acquiescence. Pessimistic determinism—the poor will always be with you but at least you can comfort them with thoughts of heaven—is much worse.

This chapter risks feeding that criticism. If it does so, it can at least quote Piketty for support. "To my knowledge," he writes:

> no society has ever existed in which ownership of capital can reasonably be described as "mildly" inegalitarian, by which I mean a distribution in which the poorest half of society would own a significant share (say, one-fifth to one-quarter) of total wealth . . . In all known societies, at all times, the least wealthy half of the population own virtually nothing . . .

Is this pessimistic determinism, or simply an honest attentiveness to reality, one that waves aside the false hopes and fairy tales that see salvation either in "market forces" (which Piketty effectively skewers) or "debate" or "democracy" or "leadership," without ever thinking carefully through the reality of each of these saviors?

Honesty should not necessitate despair, however; it acts as a solvent on optimism not on hope. A Christian response should be hopeful, not stupid. Thus much as this is the point at which this chapter should end on a stirring chorus that calls the army of Christian egalitarians to the barricades, such a chorus would be optimistic. We might not forget how Christian—dubiously Christian, perhaps, but Christian nonetheless—were the societies of Balzac and Austen and *fin de siècle* Paris and Edwardian Britain, where extreme inequality existed, seemingly impervious to objections and attempts to reduce it. There is no silver bullet of piety here.

We might, however, end on a note that takes us back to our title. The poor, Jesus tells his disciples in Matthew 26, are "always with you."

Specifically, they will always be with you "but you will not always have me." Yet the same words are used—deliberately?—in the final line of Matthew's Gospel, as the resurrected Christ, as if responding to his earlier earthly claims, this time tells his disciples "surely I am with you always, to the very end of the age" (NIV). His promise is one of presence, being with us, whatever.

"Always with you": the problem of inequality is fundamentally one of not being *with* people. Vast and/or inherited and/or unmerited differences of wealth divorce us from one another, in extreme circumstances completely and permanently, so that we get Disraeli's infamous "two nations." It was the unprecedented and threatening bringing together of radically different groups of people—Jew and Gentile, slave and free, male and female, young and old—within the earliest churches that sowed seeds that eventually and imperfectly cracked through the ineradicable inequalities of the ancient world, inequalities that went beyond the merely economic and make today's look positively gentle.

Inequality becomes harder to justify, harder to sustain, if you find yourself breaking the same bread and drinking the same wine with others you would otherwise never meet—the reason why box pews and pew rents and the practice of separate communion vessels for rich and poor is not simply a matter of cultural distance but a wholesale desecration of the gospel. At the final count, it is only here, not in the cataclysmic circumstances of war, nor in the chirpily optimistic calls for democracy or debate or leadership, but in the deep, pre-political understanding that we are called to be with one another, that we will find a political answer to the problem of inequality.

12

The Rise of Christian Populism

1

Lamenting the state of our democracy—indeed of Western liberal democracies in general—has become such a popular dinner party trope that it is almost printed on the menu now. To finish, we have coffee, petit fours, and general hand-wringing about the dangerous rise of populism in Europe and America.

There is good reason for this wailing and gnashing of teeth. Until quite recently, the global triumph of democracy seemed assured. In 1900, there were no fully fledged democracies (by today's understanding) anywhere. By 1950, 28 percent of regimes were fully democratic. Forty years later, the only apparent alternative collapsed amidst economic ruin and popular loathing, and by the year 2000 nearly two in three regimes worldwide were democratic.

The tide then appeared to turn, albeit slowly. A decade into the twenty-first century, the Economist Intelligence Unit published its regular Democracy Index, under the title *Democracy in Retreat*, remarking that "the decades-long global trend in democratisation had previously come to a halt in what Larry Diamond called a 'democratic recession.' Now democracy is in retreat." Fewer countries were making the transition to stable political accountability; more were stuck with dictatorship or worse.

No less alarming were the cluster of facts that showed how, even in those countries where democracy was apparently triumphant, its victory appeared to be hollow. Electoral turnout in Western Europe slid, from an average, two generations ago, of over 80 percent to nearer 70 percent today, and it is lower still in the US. The British got very excited by the voter turnout in 2017, especially among the young, although it remained the fifth successive General Election with a sub-70 percent turnout, lower than every post-war twentieth-century election.

Turnout for transnational or local elections is much lower still. Distrust of elected politicians and cynicism toward democratic politics have rarely been higher. Mainstream political parties have nearly died. Allegiance has fallen steadily in the post-war period, and party membership almost halved in the '80s and '90s; by the millennium, the average total party membership in a Western democracy was around 5 percent of the population, approximately a third of what it was in the 1960s. The British Labour Party under Jeremy Corbyn is the exception that proves the rule. We honor the processes and vehicles of mainstream democracy more in the breach than in our observance.

2

In the absence or, at least, decline, in mainstream democratic party politics, we have seen the rapid rise in populism.

It is dangerously easy to get pious about "populism" and to complain about it in a way that (inadvertently) explains why people turn to the populist option in the first place. This is the point of view that sees people's anxiety over immigration as nothing but covert racism; their concerns about multiculturalism as little more than xenophobia and small-mindedness; and their economic fears as simply a failure to understand that globalization is actually good for everyone in the long run. A good and intelligent friend told me in 2016 that he favored rerunning the Brexit referendum because the people who voted to leave simply didn't know what was good for them. They voted against their best interests and needed to be given an opportunity to get it right. These are explanations for populism, although not in the way they intend to be. "Populism" can sometimes sound like the name that disconcerted liberals give to the kind of politics in which ordinary people don't do what liberals tell them.

In reality, populism, like all such words, is capacious. As the *Economist* remarked, toward the end of the year in which the phenomenon came of age, the "populist" presidential candidate Donald Trump wanted to deport undocumented migrants, whereas the "populist" Spanish party Podemos wanted to give them voting rights. Bolivia's populist president, Evo Morales, expanded indigenous farmers' rights to grow coca, whilst the Philippines' populist president, Rodrigo Duterte, ordered police to execute drug dealers. In the words of the *Economist*, "Populists might be militarists, pacifists, admirers of Che Guevara or of Ayn Rand; they may be tree-hugging pipeline opponents or drill-baby-drill climate change deniers." Politically, there is very little that unites populism.

Any definition is, therefore, problematic, but I would argue that the phenomenon has three notable, and related, characteristics. One is an adherence to "the people," not in the way that all democracy does, but with a greater emphasis on the definite article in that phrase: *the* people. Populism favors rhetoric and policies that ignore or reject the plural realities of most societies and instead locates political legitimacy in the idea of a coherent, cohesive demos. In reality, that tilts them toward majoritarian politics and against ideas like human rights that undermine such politics.

The second characteristic is linked to the first; just as populism inclines away from the messy realities of pluralism toward the comforting simplicity of "the people," so it inclines away from messy compromises of representational democracy toward simple, indeed simplistic, solutions. Elites are censured (although not always, *pace* above, without reason), "experts" denounced (as Michael Gove famously did), and "radical" solutions proposed. As the *Economist* article demonstrated, the range of those solutions is vast—populism is no one-size-fits-all politics—but at its ugliest they gravitate to demonizing the other and condemning, silencing, or deporting those people (often minorities) who are allegedly at the root of the problem.

The third characteristic is linked to the first two: the rise of identity politics. "Rise" is actually the wrong term here. Identity politics has flourished for decades, albeit usually directed to minorities. Multiculturalism, a common bogeyman for populists, thrived on recognizing, fostering, protecting, and promoting identities. Populism does the same only for the majority. In this sense, populists lie in the bed that the liberals they loathe have made for them. As with the rejection of elites, it is easy to see why people take this approach—"If others are treated this way because of their ethnicity, gender, culture, or religion, then why not me?"—but it is also easy to see how this can turn ugly, a zero-sum game of identities in which yours must lose out if mine is to be affirmed.

This combination of simplicity, majoritarianism, and identity politics is a powerful one and, in particular, one to which Christians

170

should pay careful attention because Christianity has become closely tied up with it.

3

Until recently, scant attention had been paid to the role of Christianity in Western populist movements. This has been recently addressed by a fine collection of essays published by Hurst in 2016, edited by Nadia Marzouki, Duncan McDonnell, and Olivier Roy, entitled *Saving the People: How Populists Hijack Religion.*

In Italy, Poland, Switzerland, Hungary, Austria, and to a lesser or different extent Russia, Germany, the UK, and the Scandinavian countries, populist parties have drawn on Christian language, Christian imagery, and—superficially—Christian concerns. A handful of examples illustrate this. For over a decade now, Italy's Lega Nord ("Northern League") has repeatedly emphasized the defense of "the Christian people" and focused on Christian symbols in public and state spaces, seeking to protect crucifixes from the encroachment of human rights, multiculturalism, and Muslims. The Austrian Freedom Party has explicitly identified Christianity as the "spiritual foundation of Europe," spoken out against hedonistic consumption and aggressive capitalism, and launched campaigns in favor of church bells over against the Islamic Muezzin. The Swiss People's Party has campaigned vigorously against new mosques and minarets. In Hungary, Viktor Orban's governing Fidesz party and, even more so, the far right Jobbik party, have repeatedly placed stress on the need to protect Christendom against Muslims, and the evils of liberalism and multiculturalism that make straight the path for them. In America, Donald Trump was carried into power disproportionately on the (white) evangelical vote and not even—as some shamefaced Christians have liked to claim—on the nominal (white) evangelical vote. According to the Pew Forum, "Trump's support from evangelicals is strongest among those who attend church regularly [with] eight-in-ten white evangelical Protestants who attend church at least once a month approv[ing] of the way Trump is handling his job as president, including 67 percent who strongly approve of his job performance."

For these politicians, parties, and, occasionally, governments, Christianity is an immensely powerful tool. The ways in which they use it have differed subtly according to cultural context. Most talk about Europe's or America's "Christian heritage." Many talk about their "Christian roots," their "Christian values," "Christian principles," "Christian people," or "Christian identity." Some, particularly in places like Hungary that are conscious of having been on the edge of it, talk about "Christendom," although Hungarian populism mixes its Christianity with certain vaguely pagan elements. The Northern League and the Law and Justice Party have been able to play a great deal on Italy's and Poland's deeply Catholic culture, as has, to a lesser extent, Austria's Freedom Party. All of them attack the things that supposedly undermine these—capitalism occasionally, liberalism often, multiculturalism usually, Islam always.

It is important to emphasize that this isn't a necessary connection: not all populist parties and politicians are "Christian" or use Christian language and imagery. France's Front National has an ultra-conservative Catholic wing and likes to dwell on Joan of Arc and her attendant Christian symbolism as a source of national identity. However, the party has never made a specific push for Christian values, preferring instead to use the nation's *laïcité* as its rallying cry. Secularism, rather than Christianity, is used to define (and exclude) the other. Accordingly, by the reckoning of a 2010 poll in France, while 38 percent of Lutherans in Alsace cast their vote for the Front National, only 5 percent of French Evangelicals did the same.

It's a similar story in the Netherlands, where neither Pim Fortuyn List nor Geert Wilders's Freedom Party, the significant populist parties of recent years, have made any explicit appeal to Christian values or play for Christian votes. In place of others' Christianity, or France's *laïcité*, Dutch populism draws on its long-standing heritage of liberal Enlightenment values to define the people, their identity, and possible solutions. In the words of Marzouki et al., "Fortuyn evoked an ostensibly liberal heartland, but was, to so speak, intolerant of intolerant minorities."

In these countries, there is only a relatively thin Christian culture for populist politicians to weaponize; in its stead, national traditions of secularism and liberalism do the populist heavy lifting. In Greece, by contrast, the successful, hard-left Syriza Party, which rose to power on widespread anger at years of severe austerity and made populist noises in the process (at least until the reality of government began to kick in), espoused a secular approach and was led by an openly atheist politician who eschewed the traditional Orthodox blessing when assuming office. The party has maintained cordial if strained relations with the established church but clearly sees Greek Orthodoxy as part of the problem facing the country and has explored, although never systematically, the possibility of severing the state's links with the church. Given the potential for Christian-flavored populism in a country like Greece (which some minority far-right parties have adopted), the example of Syriza further underlines how the link between Christianity and populism is opportunistic rather than automatic.

4

The UK cuts a curious figure amidst these countries. It has many of the ingredients for the kind of Christian populism seen on the Continent. Levels of churchgoing may be historically low, but there remains a significant nominal cultural Christian identification, two established churches, and a strong residual attachment to "Christian values." This, combined with historically high levels of immigration and twenty years of a politically dominant multiculturalism and liberalism, creates the perfect recipe for Christian populism.

That recognized, the Christian populist movement in the UK has been anemic. By far the most successful populist party—although many of its supporters would deny it was populist at all—UKIP has been largely uninterested in playing the Christian card. Its best-known leader, Nigel Farage, has made various perfunctory Christian noises, in particular around the question of religious freedom, remarking in 2013, for example, that "it appears that this Government wishes to drive Christianity from public life." And there is also a coterie of self-consciously Christian supporters of the party called, rather directly, "Christian Soldiers of UKIP." But the party has never tried to make Christianity its own, being at least as libertarian in outlook and culture.

Before UKIP, the British National Party (BNP), with neo-fascist origins and barely concealed racism, was much more obviously populist in the terms used above. The BNP's "the people" were white and indigenous; its solutions were based on voluntary deportation of immigrants and ethnic minorities. The BNP too made one or two half-hearted attempts to hitch their political wagon to the Christian horse. In 2006, the party called for the reintroduction of morning school assemblies based on Christian worship; and a few years later, in response to a spat with the Church of England to which we will return, it ran a poster, somewhat improbably quoting Jesus from John's Gospel: "if they have persecuted me, they will also persecute you" (John 15:20). Generally speaking, however, the BNP's Christianity was thin and unpersuasive.

The only British populist party that has made a serious play—albeit an even less successful one—for the "Christian values" rhetoric so common on continental Europe is the English Defence League (EDL), an overtly racist party that moved into territory vacated by the implosion of the BNP. The EDL was (and is) aggressively anti-Muslim and uses Christian language, signs, and phrases to make its point. Its logo is a cross, of a St. George's variety, and its motto is *In hoc signo vinces*, translated as "in this sign you will conquer," the message written in the sky for the emperor Constantine before his epochal battle at the Milvian Bridge, which was the first step toward the Christianization of the Empire and of Europe.

The EDL's efforts at harnessing Christianity for its aggressively exclusionary and prejudicial politics delivered precious little success, however, and the party marks the most obviously failed attempt at a British version of Christian populism. The reason for this failure, and similarly for the BNP's, helps point toward the proper Christian response to this shift in democratic politics.

5

One oft-suggested reason why the EDL's and BNP's attempt at Christian populism failed is that there simply isn't the Christian constituency to enable it to succeed. This, however, is unconvincing, as it makes the mistake of assuming that populism draws on churchgoing Christian support as opposed to cultural Christian support. For all that some European countries (such as Poland) with Christian populist movements retain high levels of churchgoing, most others do not. In spite of the example of the US, Christian populism does not need churchgoers to work. Indeed, if the example of the French polling data cited above can be trusted, serious churchgoing may be a hindrance.

Rather, the failure of the EDL's and the BNP's Christian land grab was due in significant measure to the concerted ecclesiastical response. In the time of the latter's heyday, broadly the first decade of the century, the Church of England, Catholic Bishops Conference of England and Wales, the Methodist Church, the ecumenical instrument Churches Together in Britain and Ireland, other formal Christian organizations, and many more local ones spoke out vigorously against the BNP's politics. After the 2008 London Assembly election, in which the BNP polled over 5 percent of votes, thereby winning a seat on the Assembly, it was leaked that several Christian ministers were party members. In response, the Church of England's General Synod voted overwhelmingly in favor of banning Anglican clergy from belonging to the party—provoking the BNP's Jesus poster mentioned above.

This ecclesiastical reaction may have been notable for its concerted focus—and one must recall that, on the populist spectrum, the BNP clearly stood at the uglier, more obviously racist end—but it was not unique. Indeed, one of the features of European politics over the last decade or so has been the way in which senior church figures have stood out against Christian populism. European churches have usually and often vigorously rejected populists' overtures and often proved the most prominent critics of their calls to, for example, ban burqas, minarets, or mosques, or remove immigrants and asylum seekers. Thus, for example, in Switzerland, the Swiss People's Party "found itself at odds with the country's principal Churches . . . which considered a ban on minarets contrary to the principle of religious freedom." Next door, in a "rather explicit" press statement responding to the Austrian People's Party's official "endorsement" of Christianity in their 1997 party manifesto, the Roman Catholic Austrian Bishops Conference let it be known that it had no interest in seeing their faith used by the party in this way.

Perhaps Christian populism's biggest bête noir is Pope Francis himself. Francis chose Lampedusa, the Italian island inundated with refugees, for his first trip outside of Rome. He very publicly met with refugees housed in Lesbos. He has repeatedly spoken of the Christian duties of hospitality to the poor and needy, and not just "our" poor and needy. He has attacked the excesses of capitalism with a demotic vigor unheard from his two immediate predecessors (though his theological critique is not as different from them as many imagine).

His first encyclical was about the environment. He made some largely undisguised criticisms of Donald Trump and had a transparently terse meeting with him in May 2017. Even if he has been vocal about Europe's decline and prepared to associate it with its loss of spiritual identity, as Pope Benedict XVI repeatedly did before him, Francis's has not been the kind of "Christian Europe" message that Christian populists have liked hearing. Once again, it has been Christians who have spoken out against Christian populism.

We need to be careful here and not sugar the pill. By no means have all church leaders denounced Christian populism. Cardinal Peter Erdo, head of the Hungarian Roman Catholic Church, said that providing shelter for refugees would constitute an act of people smuggling. The Russian Orthodox Church has been central to Putin's mission of a reinvigorated Russian nation and culture and has accordingly proved his biggest supporter. Putin has aided the church's growth and prominence; restored icons, churches, and church bells; and limited the freedom of other religious groups, especially Jehovah's Witnesses and Pentecostals. The church, for its part, has proved singularly unwilling to condemn either Putin's domestic policies or his nefarious international entanglements.

One of the more dispiriting aspects of the 2016 US election was the way in which prominent church leaders fell in behind Donald Trump as it began to look like he might win the Republican nomination, all the time telling themselves and others unconvincing stories about how he had suddenly been born again on the campaign trail. At first, prominent evangelicals like James Dobson of Focus on the Family threw their weight behind Senator Ted Cruz, and according to the Pew Research Center, as late as April 2016 only a third of regular church attenders said that Trump was the preferred Republican nominee. However, Trump's Christian constituency began to swell with his success, with people like Dobson and Eric Metaxas joining Jerry Falwell Jr., president of Liberty University and long-term Trump supporter, in backing the Republican nominee. Pastor and evangelist Paula White, who was credited with leading Trump to faith and who delivered a prayer at his inauguration, insisted that she had "heard Mr. Trump verbally acknowledge his faith in Jesus Christ for the forgiveness of his sins through prayer" (although she admitted that "[he] doesn't speak what I call 'Christianese'"). Many people believed her.

In short, it has certainly not been the case that all church leaders have stood out against all populist forms of Christian appropriation. Nevertheless, the fact that and the way in which so many have points toward the critical tension that lies at the heart of Christian populism.

6

In their analysis of (primarily European) Christian populism, Marzouki, McDonnell, and Roy repeatedly stress a number of related points.

The first is that, ironically (or perhaps not), "most populists tend to be secular themselves." Christian populist politicians may well go to church—indeed, it is hard to play the Christian populist card without being seen in church. But that does not mean they have a history of churchgoing, let alone any deep spiritual, still less theological, attachment to Christianity. Neither Donald Trump nor Hungary's Viktor Orban, let alone the BNP's Nick Griffin, were reputed for their piety, in spite of their willingness to genuflect in public. This isn't a cast-iron connection—in as far as anything certain can be said of Vladimir Putin the person, it appears that his Orthodoxy is long-standing and serious. However, as a rule, Christian populist politicians aren't. Their attachment to the faith tends to the pragmatic, utilitarian, and, at its greatest extent, straightforwardly cynical.

Second, Christian populist politicians "do not consider Christianity as a faith, but rather as an identity." This is centrally important. Such politicians are profoundly interested in Christian "values," but those values tend to be wholly coterminous with the ethno-cultural-national ones of the nation or "the people" in question. In populist Hungary, for example, "God is not presented as a symbol of universal religious identity, as understood in the New Testament or explained in the speeches of Pope Francis, but as 'the God of the Hungarians,' in its particularistic, tribal, paganised political understanding." Similarly, the Austrian Freedom Party's "inclusion of religion in [its] programme ... is to be understood as a populist mobilisation strategy rather than an indicator of adherence to a faith." This is Christianity that baptizes existing national values and commitments rather than challenging them; Christianity as the priest who blesses the king rather than the prophet who challenges him. Accordingly, the level of intellectual engagement with the content of Christian faith is usually woefully thin. There is, in short, precious little theology done.

Third, the use of Christianity by populists is almost always exclusionary. Christian imagery and commitments are deployed primarily to show who is out and why, the reason being some variation of the attachment they have (or don't have) to "our" Christian culture. Inevitably, this is focused primarily on immigrants and Muslims (and especially Muslim immigrants), though it can also be used to attack those elites responsible for the liberal and multicultural policies that allow immigrants and Muslims entrance in the first place.

Fourth, they (often) "place Christendom above Christianity," or, put another way, they favor material and geographic manifestations of the faith over and above personal or relational ones. Christianity is drained of personal, spiritual content and understood, instead, primarily in territorial and political terms.

Finally, the cross—which remains a popular symbol among Christian populists—is largely "emptied" of its content. Marzouki, McDonnell, and Roy remark that "when evoking the Christian identities of their nations, populist leaders tend to refer to symbols such as the cross rather than to theological dogma." In spite of what Marzouki et al. seem to be implying here, the cross is, of course, rich and teeming with theological dogma, but their point, nonetheless, is valid: Christian populists try to ignore the "theological dogma" of the cross and instead prefer to treat it as a comfortable symbol of national or cultural identity—a kind of spiritual flag—rather than a painful and challenging symbol of sacrifice and reconciliation.

In one sense all of these points, except perhaps the first, are variations of one key problem. Christian populism pits the cause of Christian identity over and against the cause of Christian theology. The pseudo-Christian badge that stands as a cipher for my culture and nation takes precedence over its actual theological content. A Christian nation becomes a nation full of people who call themselves Christians rather than one full of people who live like Christians. Throughout, the focus is on me and others like me rather than the "other."

The division between identity and theology is not, of course, a neat and clean one. Most Christians who have some idea of what Christianity is about—let's call them "theologically literate" for want of a better phrase—are also highly likely to identify with the Christian faith. They consider themselves to hold a Christian identity and probably also to have Christian values. Those with Christian theology also have some Christian identity.

The same does not apply vice versa, however. There are many people who adhere to Christian identity who know or care little about the content of Christianity. This kind of "nominalism" is a long-standing phenomenon, even if it has become rather more widespread over recent years, to the point of being the norm in many European countries.

That recognized, its recent politicization is something new. Here we see an adherence to Christianity shorn of the content that makes the faith—or should make it—such a disconcerting presence in your life. Christian populism is a weaponized religion. Christian identity minus Christian theology allows you to speak of Christian people or Christian nation without properly scrutinizing either of those terms. It allows you to speak of Christian values without realizing how similar they are to your natural or national values. It allows you to defend Christendom without paying due attention to the problematic nature of that phenomenon. It allows you to say "no" to the other without thinking through how you might also say "yes." Ultimately, it turns Christianity into a tool for political ends, rather than making politics a tool for Christian ends.

7

Democracy abhors a theological vacuum. This doesn't mean that democracies have to be theologically literate. It doesn't mean that democracies need to call themselves Christian. It doesn't even mean that only those nations with Christian theological underpinnings will evolve into democracies, although there is a mounting body of historical-political evidence that demonstrates a clear connection between the two.

Rather, it is a deliberately provocative way of saying that democracies are made up of people, and people are naturally theological—they are, in Christian Smith's memorable formulation, "moral, believing animals." They ask profound questions about their identity, their purpose, their destiny. They are ethically conscious; they want to live good lives. They belong; they are communal, group-based, tribal.

These are the raw ingredients for some serious theological reflection, which can be done well or badly. These are also, therefore, good ingredients for populist politics, and we should not be surprised at the recent turn in that direction, after several decades of hegemonic liberalism, simultaneously playing down the attachments of majorities while cherishing those of minorities—all the time fretting about too much "belief" in politics, for fear it will deafen leaders to the demands of circumstance or the responsibilities of representation. Given these conditions, we should at least pause before passing judgement on populism, as the coffee and petit fours hit the table. There are reasons for the rise in populism, and not all of them are contemptible.

However, when populist politics hijacks Christianity, ejecting theology and replacing content in the process, Christians cannot remain silent. Secularists may seize on this trend and use it to further their cause of removing religion from the public square. But that would, in reality, be simply to exacerbate the problem. A different approach is needed. It is sometimes said that the best antidote to this bad religion is not no religion but good religion. So it is with populism: the best defense against superficial, content-lite, Christian identity politics is theologically informed, content-heavy Christian belief politics.

13

Not Just Mere Rhetoric: The Word in U.S. Politics

———•◦•———

1

The word "rhetorical" seems inexorably drawn to the word "only." If something is rhetorical, the chances are it is only rhetorical, or perhaps merely rhetorical: a figure of speech, a clever turn of phrase as opposed to a genuine belief, a thought-through idea, or a concrete action. Just as a rhetorical question is one asked to generate an effect rather than get an answer, so the rhetorical use of a text is less interested in unearthing the text's content than in using it for its rhythm or reverberations. Rhetoric is words as sounding brass and ideas as tinkling cymbals.

Many texts are plundered for their rhetorical effect, but none more so than those deemed to be authoritative. Authority here does not necessarily mean religious, despite the fact that most such "texts of authority" are religious ones. In its own way, Marx and Engels's *Communist Manifesto* was such a text, not (obviously) because of its divine sanction but because of its quasi-divine register and perspective. The *Communist Manifesto* set out the true nature of class and capital with icy logic and explained the historical inevitability of revolution. Its power might have lain in its immensely borrow-able phrasing, but its authority rested in the confidence with which it described the true nature of things, to which our impoverished reality was slowly but inexorably gravitating. A text of authority describes this true nature of reality, a vision of which our existing reality is often no more than a pale, half-adequate imitation. To use such a text rhetorically is to steal a little bit of that transcendent reality and plant it in your plot.

If authority is not necessarily connected with religion and religious texts, however, there is no doubt that it is nonetheless widely connected

181

with it, if only because you don't get much more of an authority figure than God. The Bible, supremely if not exclusively in its authorized incarnation, has been the West's foremost "text of authority," never more so than when large numbers of a population deem it sacred.

America was, and is, a fine example of this, which is why the Bible has been so widely and passionately deployed in its political rhetoric. An alien that happened to be listening in on the most recent presidential inaugural address might have been perplexed by Donald Trump's abrupt interjection to the effect that "the Bible tells us, "How good and pleasant it is when God's people live together in unity." What is this Bible, and what has it to do with the rest of his speech, our mystified Martian might ask. Indeed, why was this speaker, not famed for his recourse to this particular text, citing it at all? The answer is obvious: mere rhetoric.

If so, mere rhetoric is not a new thing. Colonists in the eighteenth century, according to Mark Noll, "drew on Scripture rhetorically—not actually to discern the will of God but more to enlist God's word on behalf of causes that may or may not have been directly taught from the sacred text." This is a severe judgment. We have already noted in an earlier chapter how biblical ideas were foundational in the political formation of America. However much eighteenth-century colonists might have polished their prose with biblical phrases, they also structured what they said on biblical lines, albeit complex, contorted, and confused ones. They may not have had regular and explicit recourse to exegesis to discern God's will for their society, in the way many of their forebears had, but nor were they indifferent to the book's content. If the Bible was the icing on their political cake, it was also one of its most important ingredients.

Moreover, the "mere rhetoric" formulation is misleading in a more profound way. The idea of "mere rhetoric" misunderstands how words and how thought works, making the assumption that the former is possible without the latter. In reality, it isn't: this is certainly true in the public sphere (and possibly, if we are to follow Wittgenstein all the way, in the private one). The public is the sphere of shared words, and the color of that language is not some kind of "rhetorical" add-on to its content. It is part of it. "My administration will respond appropriately" and "my administration will not pass by on the other side of the road" do not mean the same thing, in spite of the fact that the action in question may be the same; the biblical echo of the latter imports to its promises an ethical weight and seriousness absent in the first phrase.

The Bible can indeed be used more or less superficially in political speech but even superficial use has content, pointing to a certain understanding and framing of ideas and beliefs that has genuine import. We dismiss biblical rhetoric as "mere rhetoric" at our peril.

2

This simple idea that words change things was made in a profound way by the philosopher J. L. Austin in a series of his lectures that were subsequently published under the title *How to Do Things with Words*. Language, he argued, if delivered in the right way or by the right person or on the right occasion, could transform the material content of a situation. These are "performative utterances." Their power is usually dependent on preexisting structures of authority. The policeman says "you are under arrest"; the manager says "you're sacked"; the court clerk says "the court is in session." They speak and it is so.

Alternatively, the authority is dependent on the nature of ceremony in which the words are uttered. The dignitary says "I name this ship" at the launch. The American president says, "I do solemnly swear that I will faithfully execute the office of president..." at his inauguration. The British monarch swears "the things which I have here before promised, I will perform, and keep" at her coronation. The wife says "I will" in the marriage ceremony. Each time, reality is changed.

Reality may be altered by language in less formal and more intimate ways too. Samuel Johnson once remarked of Alexander Pope that his work exhibited "the two most engaging powers of an author. New things are made familiar, and familiar things are made new." Such is the aesthetic potential of language, bringing newness into our conceptualization of the world, whether that is the human world or, as Robert MacFarlane remarks in his book *Landmarks*, the natural one:

> Language is fundamental to the possibility of re-wonderment, for language does not just register experience, it produces it. The contours and colour of words are inseparable from the feelings we create in relation to situations, to others and to places. Language carries a formative as well as an informative impulse.

Political words have the same power. Formally, they can start wars—such as when Neville Chamberlain took to the airwaves at 11:15 a.m. on September 3, 1939, to indicate that Britain was now "at war with Germany." Or they can start countries, the US Constitution arguably being, in philosopher Charles Taylor's words, "a long performative [utterance] in which a collective subject, identified in the beginning as 'We, the people of the United States,' declares the Constitution in effect."

Less formally still, they can bring about the sense of collective identity on which nations, and states, and political movements, and even revolutions are erected in the first place. This is precisely what they have done in American history, and it is precisely what the Bible has done in American history.

3

As noted in an earlier chapter, the Bible was everywhere in pre-Revolutionary America. In a study of American political rhetoric from 1760 to 1805 (a study that excluded 90 percent of sermons, a great many of which were political), the political scientist Donald S. Lutz found that the Bible was referred to more often than any European writer or European school of thought, comprising a third of all references. As late as the 1770s and '80s, nearly 80 percent of all political pamphlets were written by ministers.

Pre-Revolutionary America, and in particular New England, was a comparatively literate society; indeed it was a comparatively biblically literate one. In 1781, Benjamin Franklin wrote from France to Rev. Dr. Samuel Cooper, pastor of a prominent Boston church, thanking him for a sermon he had sent him. Franklin said that he intended to translate the sermon for his European audience but that he would need to insert biblical references for that audience that were not necessary for the US one. "I have observed in England as well as in France," he said, "that Verses and Expressions taken from the sacred Writings, and not known to be such, appear very strange and awkward to some readers."

The political use of Scripture was, of course, nothing new. Indeed, it was wholly in keeping with the text itself. As the theologian Oliver O'Donovan once observed, almost the whole core vocabulary of the New Testament—including words like salvation, justification, peace, faithfulness, and redemption—had political prehistory of some kind. To appropriate the Bible for political ends was hardly a misappropriation. It was almost impossible for words like rights, dis/loyalty, tyranny, order, representation, and rebellion to avoid biblical echoes. The revolutionaries spoke Bible just as assuredly as they spoke English.

What they said with it, however, was less straightforward. Indeed, one of the reasons why so much credence is given to the idea of "mere rhetoric" is that the Bible was used on both sides of the argument. We may remember the revolutionaries most readily, but we shouldn't forget the loyalists, nor their use of the Bible to justify their loyalty to crown and parliament. Naturally, those authoritarian-sounding texts, much favored by the early Reformers, played a key role in their arguments. Romans 13:1–7 stated baldly that "whosoever therefore resisteth the power, resisteth the ordinance of God," and 1 Peter 2:13–17 commanded that Christians "submit yourselves to every ordinance of man for the Lord's sake: whether it be to the king, as supreme; or unto governors." With such clear, unambiguous, and blunt demands for loyalty and admonitions against rebellion, what more was needed?

Some have argued that the loyalists "lacked the flare for analogizing ancient Israel that patriotic ministers mastered," but if that were true it was, in large measure, because so much of the life of ancient Israel was lived in opposition and resistance—to Egypt, to Assyria, to Babylon, to its own self-serving rulers. The biblical model naturally oriented colonists toward opposition and, in any case, the rhetoric of change, of reformation, of revolution is usually more powerful than that of stasis. Accordingly, the revolutionaries picked up the word and used it.

They undermined not only the practice but the institution of kingship, by means of the prophet Samuel's principled arguments against kingship in 1 Samuel 8 and through the strict demands laid upon kings in Deuteronomy 17 (demands that George III did not meet), and, naturally, through the litany of corrupt kings and venal officials charted in the books of Kings.

They analogized the new colonies to the tribes of Israel, skirting around the slightly numerical mismatch in the process. The Congregational clergyman Samuel Langdon declared in a 1788 election sermon entitled "The Republic of the Israelites an Example to the American States" that "instead of the twelve tribes of Israel, we may substitute the thirteen States of the American union."

They lifted verses lock, stock, and barrel. This was sometimes to justify their rebellion, such as Galatians 5:1, which states, "Stand fast therefore in the liberty wherewith Christ hath made us free, and be not entangled again with the yoke of bondage," or Acts 5:29, which reads, "We ought to obey God rather than men." Elsewhere, it was sometimes to warn themselves of their divine responsibility, especially Micah 6:8: "what doth the LORD require of thee, but to do justly, and to love mercy, and to walk humbly with thy God?" and Psalm 33:12: "Blessed is the nation whose God is the LORD; and the people whom he hath chosen for his own inheritance."

And they made repeated reference to the story of the Exodus, the colonists seeing England as an Egypt of political and religious tyranny from which they fled, George III its intransigent Pharaoh, the perilous Atlantic Ocean their Red Sea, George Washington their Moses, and America their Canaan. Dreisbach tells us that George Washington, somewhat circumspect about his own faith, was particularly fond of the metaphor of vines and figs. He wrote to a friend in January 1783, for example, "I wish you may possess health and spirits to enjoy, after we shall have seated ourselves under our own Vines and Fig trees, if it is the gracious will of Providence to permit it, the return of many happy years."* Washington was a keen gardener, after a fashion, but his wishes,

---

* A parenthesis: "vines and figs" are a useful way of undermining one of the most persistent misunderstandings when it comes to biblical language. It is common today to hear the accusation (and it usually is an accusation) that Christians take the Bible "literally" (which means they are "biblical literalists," which means they are "fundamentalists," which means they are mad, bad, and dangerous to know). This is usually placed in opposition to a "metaphorical" reading, which is sounder, softer, and safer. It is either/or.

How about this phrase? How should we read the common Old Testament promise pertaining to vines and figs, most famously articulated by the prophet Micah: "But they shall sit every man under his vine and under his fig tree; and none shall make them afraid." Is this literal or metaphorical? On reflection, it is—indeed it can only be—both. The prophets spoke of vines and figs because they offer sustenance, sweetness, and shade. They spoke of growing them because to be able to do so meant having sufficient political security over a sufficiently long time to plant, tend, and harvest them (you don't nurture vines and figs in a war zone). And they spoke of "each man" owning their

186

here and elsewhere, were not primarily horticultural. They were part of the wider rhetorical ploy of embedding the nascent nation in a biblical narrative. Indeed, America came perilously close to having the Exodus as the mark of its national seal, as, when the Continental Congress appointed Thomas Jefferson, Benjamin Franklin, and John Adams to a committee to design a seal for the newly declared independent nation on July 4, 1776, Franklin proposed an image of Moses extending his hand over the parting Red Sea.

4

The idea that all this was "mere" rhetoric—that there was limited depth or integrity to the colonists' use of the Bible—is based on (at least) three powerful foundations: the different ends to which it was used, the way in which it was used, and the people by whom it was used.

The first of these is the most obvious. The simple fact is that the Bible could be and was used on both sides of the debate. The Scriptures were the heavy weaponry deployed once the battle lines had already been drawn, but they played little role in the strategic organization of the war (metaphorically—but also literally—speaking).

Apparently a knockdown argument, this is less impressive than it first seems. The Bible was indeed hauled onto existing battle lines but, as already intimated, that was partly because it had already had centuries of involvement in the more strategic task of working out the positions. Loyalists and revolutionaries were not citing the Bible to gild their arguments in some kind of shallow, opportunistic, or arbitrary way. The former genuinely believed the Scriptures endorsed (unquestioning) loyalty to the powers that were in London; the latter believed that it mandated rebellion against them because those powers were no longer serving God in justice but had become tyrannous.

One might complain that the Bible itself allowed these various colonists to adopt such a range of positions, but the Bible, as I have

---

own vines because to do so meant there was a reasonable level of economic equity and justice, and that each household was therefore reasonably financially secure. The political and economic implications of the metaphor only have purchase because of the literal, material things on which the metaphorical use is based.

argued elsewhere,* is a plurivocal political text, adept at being mis- or, rather, too narrowly, heard. The fact that certain colonists heard, or heeded, only one message may reflect a thin political theology but not the conclusion that their usage was "merely" rhetorical.

5

The second argument, pertaining to the way the Bible was used, is similarly problematic. Daniel Dreisbach has done a commendable job of categorizing the range of theo-political rhetoric of the revolutionaries, an adapted selection of which is outlined below.

The first is all but unconscious—the use of biblical phrases simply because they had passed into the linguistic bloodstream: "forbidden fruit," "fat of the land," "seven times seven years," "thorn in our side," "first fruit," "neither sleep nor slumber," "like sheep to the slaughter," "engraved on every man's heart," "separating the Wheat from the Tares," "a millstone hung to your neck," "wars and rumors of wars," "take up my bed and walk," "widow's mite," etc. If anything is "mere rhetoric" it is this, but even here one needs to be cautious, as it is not always straightforward to tell whether the phrase in question is deployed with intent or not.

Second is the use of distinctively biblical allusions or figures of speech consciously "to enrich a common language and cultural vocabulary," but not, apparently, to make any substantive point. In this fashion, Washington wrote to the German Lutherans of Philadelphia, in April 1789, shortly before assuming the presidency, saying, "I flatter myself [that] opportunities will not be wanting for me to shew my disposition to encourage the domestic and public virtues of industry, economy, patriotism, philanthropy, and that righteousness which exalteth a nation" (the final phrase is from Prov. 14:34). This might be rhetorical, but it is clearly more deliberate, and weightier, than many of the phrases of the previous paragraph.

A third category is similar but more substantive, the Bible being used to enhance what is being said, authorizing, blessing, or sanctifying the ordinary (or extraordinary) business of politics. In Daniel Dreisbach's

---

* See Nick Spencer, *Freedom and Order: History, Politics and the English Bible* (London: Hodder & Stoughton, 2011).

words, "Arousing a righteous passion, solemnifying a discourse, projecting an aura of transcendence and truth, emphasizing the gravity of an idea or argument, and/or underscoring an argument's moral implications or sacred connotations": the Bible was endlessly useful for those revolutionaries who wanted to lift their endeavors on to a higher, religious plain.

Fourth, and more substantive still, the Bible was used normatively, plundered "to identify and define . . . standards and transcendent rules for ordering and judging public life." This was rhetoric as exegesis, studying the Scriptures for models, precedents, lessons, warnings, and commands that would shape the Revolutionaries' political endeavors. In his *Reading the Bible with the Founding Fathers*, Dreisbach gives the example of how, in the last days of the Constitutional Convention, during debate on a proposal to require the ownership of property as a qualification for public office under the Constitution, Benjamin Franklin spoke in opposition to any proposal "that tended to debase the spirit of the common people. . . . We should remember the character which the Scripture requires in Rulers," he said, invoking Jethro's qualifications for prospective Israelite rulers in Exodus 18:21, that they should be "men of truth, hating covetousness." The speech, Dreisbach notes, is "a rare instance in the Constitutional Convention when a delegate cited biblical authority in support of a specific constitutional provision."

Such a categorization makes it abundantly clear that there were indeed more and less substantive, more and less deliberate, more and less thoughtful uses of the Bible in revolutionary rhetoric. The closer one gets toward the end of this list, the more obvious it is that the Bible was being used to decide rather than decorate politics.

However, even the less substantive/deliberate/thoughtful uses— the more obviously "rhetorical" ones—cannot be simply dismissed as mere rhetoric, for implicitly their use says "this is the people we are" and "this is the goal we are pursuing," and, more powerfully still, "this is the narrative we are inhabiting" and "this is the direction in which Providence is leading us." Loose, general "mere" rhetoric helped delineate a people, its history, its rights, its obligation, and its destiny.

Such messages were immensely powerful, perhaps even more powerful for being implicit. They served as a kind of informal speech-act to match the formal speech-act of the Constitution. Just as the latter was, in Charles Taylor's words, from his book *The Language Animal,* "a long performative [utterance] in which a collective subject . . . 'We, the people' . . . declares the Constitution in effect," so the biblical rhetoric of the Revolutionaries subtly created a concept of who these people were in the first place.

6

The final "mere rhetoric" argument gains force from the question of who employed the biblical speech. We might give credence to Benjamin Rush, John Adams, or John Witherspoon for their use of the Bible, being the devout and biblicist public figures they were. We might even grant it to those like George Washington, who were (probably) devout but rather more privately so. Yet can we really see heartfelt biblical use from the pen of heterodox, deistic, anticlerical, lukewarm, or frankly antagonistic figures like Benjamin Franklin, Thomas Jefferson, and Thomas Paine?

Such figures did in fact talk Bible. Paine reveled in biblical allusions: to the order of creation, to the corrupt Old Testament monarchy, to Samuel's disapproval of government by kings, to the tyrannous Herod. Jefferson drew on the comparison between America and the Children of Israel, closing his second inaugural address in March 1805 by encouraging all Americans to join him in seeking "the favour of that Being in whose hands we are, who led our forefathers, as Israel of old, from their native land, and planted them in a country flowing with all the necessaries and comforts of life."

There is clearly some merit in the argument that, knowing what we do of them, when such Founding Fathers quoted Scripture they were, at best, simply gilding their real arguments; at worst, they were engaged in hypocrisy and an early form of media-management. Once again, however, this argument is not persuasive.

First, no matter how anticlerical they were, such founders expressed sincere and deep-felt admiration for Jesus and, in particular, his teachings. They may have doubted that he was the Son of God, but they never imagined his teachings were irrelevant, still less dangerous, to people. The Bible—or at very least bits of it—mattered, even if it was not infallible revelation.

Second, as good, classically educated republicans, the deistic Founding Fathers believed that successful republican government needed national virtue and national virtue needed religious anchoring. Their denial of the truth of revelation steered them toward natural religion, much of which, they believed in any case, was evident in the pages of Scripture. Nevertheless, once again, there was precious little sense that religion was irrelevant or dangerous to contemporary life—quite the contrary, in fact.

Third, and most significantly, they were conscious of speaking to a devoutly Christian people. Even if it wasn't now their natural tongue—despite having once been for some, like Franklin and Paine, their mother tongue—"Bible" was still the lingua franca, by means of which the people were both formed and informed. Whatever the deepest motives, and however cynical it might have been, there was nothing "mere" about their biblical rhetoric.

Overall, the very fact (a) that political community could be addressed in the same biblical terms as were used to address the church, and (b) that the story of ancient Israel—captivity, promise, liberation, and covenant—could be deployed as a master narrative for the revolutionaries' cause served as an immensely powerful motivating force for the new nation. All in all, whilst the ends to which it was used, the way in which it was used, and the people by whom it was used could make the biblical rhetoric of the Revolution seem more superficial, or "rhetorical," to dismiss it as mere rhetoric, in the sense of not mattering very much, is a mistake. The Bible was a powerful weapon, however it was used.

7

It remained so well into the twentieth century. Indeed, one of the most striking and impressive examples of such biblical "rhetoric" can be seen in that most notoriously "secular" of decades, the 1960s, through the voice of Martin Luther King Jr. and the civil rights movement.

King dwelt heavily on biblical motifs, drawing liberally from Hebrew prophets like Amos and Isaiah, in his quest for "justice and righteousness" to "level mountains" and "make crooked places straight." His best-known motif was the Exodus, which he repeatedly used to frame and narrate the civil rights movement.

In the last speech of his life, in Memphis, Tennessee, King dwelt famously on the Israelites' entry into Canaan and, at greater length, on the parable of the Good Samaritan. The parable was used to exhort the crowd to "develop a kind of dangerous unselfishness." Whereas the priest and the Levite had, motivated by fear, asked the question, "If I stop to help this man, what will happen to me?," the Samaritan, motivated by love, asked, "If I do not stop to help this man, what will happen to him?" Canaan, in contrast, was used to reassure the audience that their "dangerous unselfishness" would triumph in the end. God had allowed him to go up to the mountain and see the Promised Land, and live (and die) in the knowledge that "we, as a people" will get there.

In this way, King's Memphis speech, like so many of his other speeches, deployed the Bible, and especially the Exodus narrative, to adduce unity, cooperation, confidence, discipline, peacefulness, perseverance, and hope in a movement that was under severe pressure to abandon them all. In the words of Gary Selby's *Martin Luther King and the Rhetoric of Freedom: The Exodus Narrative in America's Struggle for Civil Rights,* "By symbolically framing their experiences within a deeply held religious myth—one that had been traditionally used to create expectations for social change—he could offer a theological justification for engaging in collective action."

Things were changing in American political life by the time King made his speech, which would result in a subtly different, and rather more problematic, deployment of the word. To understand these, we need briefly to go back from April 1968 to the early years of the nation to trace the story of the intervening years.

8

For all the towering edifice it has become, Thomas Jefferson's "Wall of Separation" started life as more of a low fence.

As James Hutson says in his *Church and State in America,* "to claim or imply that the Declaration of Independence ignited a headlong, nationwide effort to sever the ligaments between government and religion is simply not true." When Vermont became, in 1791, the first state after the original thirteen colonies admitted to the Union, seven of the nation's (now fourteen) states authorized some form of establishment of religion by law.

These connections were slowly untangled over the next half century, not least by devout believers themselves who, especially in the wake of the Second Great Awakening, became increasingly disaffected with the "public utility" argument for religion that underpinned so much establishment thought. Jefferson's now famous letter to the Danbury Baptists (although not famous at the time: the letter did not even make it into the first edition of Jefferson's *Collected Works*) has been read as part of this disentangling, and indeed as a secular ideological driver behind it. In reality, as he informed his attorney general in 1802, the letter was specifically intended to explain "why I do not proclaim fastings & thanksgivings, as my predecessors did." When his predecessor, John Adams, had proclaimed a national day of fasting in March 1798, he had been accused of scheming to impose a (Presbyterian) establishment on the nation (despite the fact that he was not in fact a Presbyterian). Adams later claimed that the ensuing furor helped him lose the 1800 presidential election. Nothing, he said, "is more dreaded than the national government meddling with religion."

Jefferson, in the Danbury letter, was defending his decision not to fall into Adams's error and, more broadly, defending himself against the Federalists' accusations of godlessness. Deleted and blotted-out sections of the letter, recovered by the FBI in 1998, have Jefferson explaining the difference between a British monarch and an American president with reference to the ancient distinction, attributed to the fifth-century pope Gelasius, between spiritual and temporal authority. Whereas the British king combined these roles in his person, the American president did not, and should not. The Bill of Rights, by Jefferson's reckoning, debarred the president from officiating in any spiritual matters. Hence his letter to the Baptists was intended not as part of the secular magisterium delivered, as it were, ex cathedra, but as a defense of himself and of the republic. In reality, the First Amendment and Jefferson's Wall of Separation were intended to sever religion's political mandate and politics' religious mandate from one another, not to excise religion from political thought and rhetoric altogether. In Hutson's words:

> the [first] amendment was intended by Madison and his fellow drafters to make explicit the small *f* federalism on which the Constitution was grounded... All indications are that in debating the religion clause of ...

the First Amendment, Congress only considered the issue of federalism as it related to the propriety of religious taxes levied by the New England state government.

Nearly a century and a half later, the Supreme Court decided that language of the First Amendment, prohibiting Congress from making laws establishing a religion, applied to the states and brought their religious practices under the scrutiny of the federal courts. In 1947, the Supreme Court sought to use Jefferson's Danbury letter in *Everson v. Board of Education*, which was about constitutionality of public reimbursement of bus fares of students attending Catholic schools. The Court upheld the reimbursement but spoke of Jefferson's Wall of Separation being "high and impregnable" in what was to be a precedent-setting way. The following year, engaging in a rather dubious exercise of "jurisprudence of original intention" in *McCollum v. Board of Education*, the Court "constitutionalized" Jefferson's Wall by asserting it was the correct interpretation of the First Amendment's establishment clause (in spite the fact that it wasn't about the Constitution, which had been written thirteen years earlier, when Jefferson had been in France). The wall would subsequently be invoked to strike down other practices that allegedly threatened the separation of church and state, like prayer, Bible-reading in schools, and other low-key Christian activities in public spaces.

The result was a source of much joy and hope to America's then small secular minority, as the public square was gradually evacuated of religious content. It was only partially successful and didn't stop Congress from passing a bill that added the words "under God" to the nation's Pledge of Allegiance in 1954, or President Eisenhower from making "In God We Trust" the national motto in 1956, as part of the nation's assertion of godly identity in the face of the atheistic Soviet threat. Nor, self-evidently, did it drain public rhetoric of religious content or silence Martin Luther King's Scripture-soaked rhetoric. It did, however, begin to polarize American political, cultural, and rhetorical life around religious lines in a way that hadn't happened before, as some Americans clung to this more muscular secularism and sneered at those who liked to quote chapter and verse, while others, first smarted at what they saw as an illegitimate denuding of the public square, began fighting back.

9

And fight back they did. In their book on religious rhetoric in recent American politics, *The God Strategy: How Religion Became a Political Weapon in America*, David Domke and Kevin Coe showed how, between Franklin D. Roosevelt in the 1930s and Jimmy Carter in the 1970s, around a half of White House addresses to the nation invoked God, from high points of FDR himself and Truman, at about 60 percent, to a low point of Nixon and Carter, at 30 percent. When Ronald Reagan captured the evangelical (and, to some extent, Catholic) vote from Carter—winsomely telling an evangelical meeting in 1980: "I know this is non-partisan, so you can't endorse me, but I want you to know that I endorse you"—everything changed. Reagan invoked God in 96 percent of his White House addresses to the nation. After him, the figure hasn't fallen below 90 percent.

A similar story could be told of the number of times God was invoked in such addresses. This hovered between one and two, between 1933 and 1981, but then increased to an average of three with Reagan. More tellingly, in what Domke and Coe call "high state occasions," such as inaugural and State of the Union addresses, the increase went from between one and three on average, from FDR to Carter, to six with Reagan.

In such speeches, the same pattern emerged with more general invocations of faith and use of the language of mission and crusade. Invocations of God's help and general requests for divine favor, for example, oscillated between 10 and 40 percent, between FDR and Gerald Ford, and fell to under 10 percent for Carter, but they shot up to over 90 percent with Reagan.

Perhaps most tellingly, prior to Reagan taking office, the phrase "God bless America" had, remarkably, been used only once in national addresses, by Nixon on April 30, 1973 (as he concluded a speech about Watergate). After 1980, it became a staple of virtually every major US presidential speech. Domke and Coe concluded that "it's not that explicit language about God entered the presidency in 1981; it's that with Reagan explicit language about God became publicly embedded in the presidency—and, by extension, in US politics." The rhetorical Word was resurgent.

In all of these instances, even extending to Donald Trump's biblical parenthesis in his inaugural address after the most toxic and divisive campaign in modern times, the object of the "godly" or biblical rhetoric was to unify, strengthen, inspire, guide, or comfort the nation. And yet by this point, so divided was the nation, and so entangled with questions of religion, Bible, and secularism had those divisions become, that what the rhetorical Word had once achieved under the Founding Fathers or Dr. King—change, justice, healing—seemed a now impossible goal.

Republicans "did God," to use the phrase made famous by Tony Blair's press secretary, and they talked God, and they did so confidently. Democrats either didn't do him, or they did so quietly, at pains to emphasize that their faith might have been personal but was also private. They made political decisions based on reason rather than faith. They ran to be, for example, the senator from Illinois rather than the minister of Illinois.

There were moments when both Republicans and Democrats tried to transcend this divide. In a famous 2006 speech on faith and politics, Obama said that "the discomfort of some progressives with any hint of religion has often prevented us from effectively addressing issues in moral terms." By erasing God-talk from political language, "we forfeit the imagery and terminology through which millions of Americans understand both their personal morality and social justice."

Such attempts, however, also served to underline the depth of that divide. Michael Wear, Barack Obama's faith outreach director in 2008 and 2012, tells a story of how Pastor Rick Warren invited then-Senator Obama and Senator Sam Brownback, a conservative Catholic from Kansas, to the World AIDS Day Summit 2006. Brownback opened his remarks by referring to a previous meeting between them, in the process implying that whereas that previous meeting at the NAACP was among "Obama's people," this one, at evangelical Warren's Saddleback church, was with Brownback's. He concluded with the words, "Welcome to my house." Obama's reply was simultaneously a slap-down and an attempt to build a bridge: "There is one thing I have to say, Sam. This is my house. This is God's house."

Obama's first presidential campaign was a hopeful moment for bridging this rhetorical chasm. His second one was rather less so and, by Wear's retelling, thereafter Democrats returned to a secular, and for some even anti-faith, comfort zone.

10

Hebrews 4:12 is a famous verse. In the rich translation with which the Founding Fathers would have been familiar it tells us that "the word of God is quick, and powerful, and sharper than any twoedged sword, piercing even to the dividing asunder of soul and spirit, and of the joints and marrow, and is a discerner of the thoughts and intents of the heart."

This, unlike Micah's vines and figs, is more obviously pure metaphor and open to various interpretations. The word of God, the Scriptures, can challenge the reader. It can look into and judge your soul. It can change your life. Being a double-edged sword is more than usually dangerous, able to mount an attack from several angles and in many more ways than a single-edged sword, but it also increases the danger to the person who is wielding it. It is dangerous.

And so its use in American political history has shown. From the earliest times it has been used rhetorically to challenge, undermine, and defy authorities as well as to unify, strengthen, and comfort a nation. But it has rarely been used merely rhetorically. Indeed, it is very hard to use it merely rhetorically. Perhaps that is the reason why some secularists tried to sheath it in the latter decades of the twentieth century. As it turned out, it was not a sensible tactic. Double-edged swords, whether you wield them or sheath them, are dangerous weapons.

Further Reading

———•◦•———

The above chapters refer to, draw on, and quote from a number of books. Because the book is not itself intended to be a work of scholarship, I have on the whole refrained from foot and endnotes throughout. However, I would like to highlight the most significant texts on which the chapters are based, and which the reader might wish to consult for further reflection on the questions under discussion in this book.

Chapter 1 ("Why the West Is Different") is an extended review of Larry Siedentop's *Inventing the Individual: The Origins of Western Liberalism* (London: Allen Lane, 2014); **Chapter 10** ("The Secular Self") is an essay review of Charles Taylor's *A Secular Age* (Cambridge, MA: Belknap, 2007); **Chapter 11** ("'Always with You'") is an essay-review of Thomas Piketty's *Capital in the Twenty-First Century*, trans. Arthur Goldhammer (Cambridge, MA: Harvard/Belknap, 2014).

Chapter 2 ("Religiously Secular") and **Chapter 13** ("Not Just Mere Rhetoric") draw on Mark Noll, *In the Beginning Was the Word: The Bible in American Public Life, 1492–1783* (New York: Oxford University Press, 2015); Daniel Dreisbach, *Reading the Bible with the Founding Fathers* (New York: Oxford University Press, 2016); James Hutson, *Church and State in America: The First Two Centuries* (New York: Cambridge University Press, 2008); David Domke and Kevin Coe, *The God Strategy: How Religion Became a Political Weapon in America* (New York: Oxford University Press, 2008); and John Coffey, *Exodus and Liberation: Deliverance Politics from John Calvin to Martin Luther King Jr.* (New York: Oxford University Press, 2014). I am grateful to John Coffey and Andy Crouch for their very helpful feedback on both of these chapters.

Chapter 3 ("Trouble with the Law") and **Chapter 5** ("Saving Humanism from the Humanists") draw on Theos publications, respectively *The Church and the Charter: Christianity and the Forgotten Roots of the Magna Carta* by Thomas Andrew (2015), and *The Case for Christian Humanism: Why Christians Should Believe in Humanism and Humanists* *in Christianity*, by myself and Angus Ritchie (2014). Both reports are available at https://www.theosthinktank.co.uk/.

Chapter 4 ("Christianity and Democracy") draws on my own *Freedom and Order: History, Politics and the English Bible* (London: Hodder & Stoughton, 2011); Chapter 6 ("Christianity and Atheism") is derived from my *Atheists: The Origin of the Species* (London: Bloomsbury Continuum, 2013); Chapter 8 ("'No Doubts as to How One Ought to Act'") from my *Darwin and God* (London: SPCK, 2009).

Chapter 7 ("The Accidental Midwife") draws on Stephen Gaukroger's *The Emergence of a Scientific Culture: Science and the Shaping of Modernity 1210–1685* (Oxford: Clarendon, 2006) and on Peter Harrison's work, especially *The Territories of Science and Religion* (Chicago: University of Chicago Press, 2015).

Chapter 9 ("The Religion of Christianity and the Religion of Human Rights") makes close reference to Samuel Moyn's *Christian Human Rights* (Philadelphia: University of Pennsylvania Press, 2015) and to Nicholas Wolterstorff's *Justice: Rights and Wrongs* (Princeton, NJ: Princeton University Press, 2010).

Chapter 12 ("The Rise of Christian Populism") draws on Nadia Marzouki, Duncan McDonnell, and Olivier Roy, eds., *Saving the People: How Populists Hijack Religion* (London: C. Hurst & Co. Publishers, Ltd., 2016).

Index

CPSIA information can be obtained
at www.ICGtesting.com
Printed in the USA
LVHW101055250722
724313LV00011B/107